Endorsements for the Conversational Commentaries Series

"This is the series I've been waiting for! These Conversational Commentaries are for every Bible study leader, small group facilitator, Bible teacher, and Bible study participant. Written by women, for women, these volumes help you engage deeply with Scripture, equip you for rich discussions, deepen your understanding of God's word, and point you to Christ."

Courtney Doctor, Director of Women's Initiatives, The Gospel Coalition; Bible teacher; author, *From Garden to Glory* and *In View of God's Mercies*

"The Conversational Commentaries series is a trusted companion for individual study or teacher preparation. I appreciate each author's careful consideration of the original writer, document, and audience while keeping the language and format refreshingly accessible. These handy reference tools will be great additions to any theological library to return to repeatedly."

Karen Hodge, Coordinator of Women's Ministries, Presbyterian Church in America; coauthor, *Transformed: Life-Taker to Life-Giver* and *Life-Giving Leadership*

"For those looking for an accessible and theologically robust commentary series, start here. These commentaries are informed, responsible, and God glorifying."

Benjamin L. Gladd, Executive Director, The Carson Center for Theological Renewal

"These commentaries are indeed 'conversational,' but they are not without great theological depth and exegetical rigor. I'm so grateful for these dear sisters in Christ—for their biblical wisdom, love for God's word and God's people, and desire to help fellow women of God dig into the glorious riches of Scripture. Many thanks to Lydia Brownback and Megan Hill for their editing of these immensely valuable resources!"

Jon Nielson, Founding Pastor, Christ Presbyterian Church, Wheaton, Illinois

"Of the two ways to get into the ocean, wading in from a beach is preferable to being dropped in from a helicopter. If you're not sure where to start in your study of the Bible, Conversational Commentaries will help guide you into the deep truths of God's word step by step. Why stay on the shore?"

Gloria Furman, author, *Labor with Hope* and *Missional Motherhood*

"This is the commentary series I wish I'd had when I started teaching the Bible. Trusted authors offer sound and accessible content for those wanting to deepen their study or strengthen their teaching. Whether you're new to studying the Bible or you've studied it for years, you want this series in your library."

Colleen D. Searcy, speaker; Bible teacher; author, Meet Me in the Bible study series

"Faithful, relatable, practical—Conversational Commentaries are the first books to pull off the shelf when you need to understand or teach the Bible, passage by passage. Equally valuable for personal study or public witness, the simple yet profound titles in this new series empower godly women to know, apply, and teach the Bible in life-changing ways."

Philip Graham Ryken, President, Wheaton College

"These Conversational Commentaries absolutely deliver what they promise. They read like a wise friend sitting across the table explaining the text verse by verse, answering the questions that most naturally arise. While they offer sound scholarship, they eschew an overly academic tone. And while they ably cover the entire text, they are helpfully concise. I will pull these volumes off my shelf again and again."

Nancy Guthrie, author; Bible teacher

Ephesians

Conversational Commentaries

Edited by Lydia Brownback and Megan Hill

Theological Review by Douglas Sean O'Donnell

Ephesians: Life Together in Christ, Megan Hill

1 Peter: Hope for Exiles, Lydia Brownback

Ephesians

Life Together in Christ

Megan Hill

CROSSWAY®

WHEATON, ILLINOIS

Portions of "Overview: The New Testament Epistles" have been adapted from Lydia Brownback, *1–2 Peter: Living Hope in a Hard World* (Crossway, 2021). Used by permission.

Cover illustration and design: Jordan Singer

First printing 2026

Printed in China

Trade paperback ISBN: 978-1-4335-9905-7
ePub ISBN: 978-1-4335-9907-1
PDF ISBN: 978-1-4335-9906-4

Library of Congress Cataloging-in-Publication Data

Names: Hill, Megan, 1978– author
Title: Ephesians : life together in Christ / Megan Hill.
Description: Wheaton, Illinois : Crossway, [2026] | Includes bibliographical references and index.
Identifiers: LCCN 2025036357 (print) | LCCN 2025036358 (ebook) | ISBN 9781433599057 paperback | ISBN 9781433599071 ebook | ISBN 9781433599064 pdf
Subjects: LCSH: Bible. Ephesians—Study and teaching | Bible. Ephesians—Criticism, interpretation, etc. | Christian life—Biblical teaching
Classification: LCC BS2695.55 .H55 2026 (print) | LCC BS2695.55 (ebook)
LC record available at https://lccn.loc.gov/2025036357
LC ebook record available at https://lccn.loc.gov/2025036358

For Christina, Loren, Nina, Samantha, and Sarah

Thank you for studying and teaching Ephesians with me—
you have helped me grow up into Christ (Eph. 4:15).

Contents

Series Preface

So, you have a hunger for God's word. We know that's true because you've picked up this little commentary. Whatever your goal—diving deep on your own or leading a small-group Bible study—Conversational Commentaries are designed to serve as a companion in your study of Scripture.

There is no shortage of Bible commentaries, but this series offers something unique. Every volume is authored by a woman and has female readers in view as it explains and applies the biblical text. These volumes are *conversational*: Each author writes as though she is talking with friends over mugs of coffee and open Bibles. Every volume is also a *commentary*: a verse-by-verse explanation of one book of the Bible. Here you'll discover that every word of Scripture is more valuable than gold and sweeter than honey (Ps. 19:10)—and each verse is one you can understand and apply with the Spirit's help. Each Conversational Commentary is an accessible, affordable resource that provides depth and detail for women who want to grow in their knowledge of God's word. Although these books don't focus on academic terms or technical details about the original text, they will help you study the Bible in all its richness. These commentaries present sound biblical scholarship in language that any Christian can understand. It's our hope that this series would help you grow in your knowledge of God's word, in your ability to study and teach it to others, and—ultimately—in your love for Christ, to whom all Scripture points.

How to Use This Series

As part of your daily, personal Bible study. While you're reading the Scriptures devotionally, these commentaries will help you understand and apply the verses (especially the confusing ones!) and see how they fit into the larger context of the chapter and book.

As a textbook for a small-group study. Each person in the group can read the commentary along with the assigned Scripture text, and you can discuss what you've learned when you meet together.

As research material for Bible teaching. Whether you're being called on to give a quick devotional or teach an entire book of the Bible, these commentaries will help you prepare to lead others through Scripture.

As a tool for evangelistic one-on-one Bible reading. When you're meeting with an unbeliever to walk through Scripture, these commentaries can help you answer questions about even the most difficult text.

As a resource for family worship. As you study the Bible with the people in your home, these commentaries will give you simple language to explain and discuss each verse.

As a book of answers to your Bible questions. When you are scratching your head about the meaning of a particular verse or idea in Scripture, these commentaries provide a bite-sized explanation.

LYDIA BROWNBACK AND MEGAN HILL

Overview

The New Testament Epistles

Before we dive into this letter, it's vital to say a general word about how to study the Epistles, which make up much of the New Testament. The Epistles teach about salvation in Christ Jesus and how we're called to live out our faith in day-to-day life. Because they were written to believers in the time after Christ's resurrection and ascension, the Epistles are some of the easiest books of the Bible for us to read. We feel a kinship with the original audience because they were in a situation similar to ours: They had believed the truth of Christ's death and resurrection, received the gift of his Spirit, and were seeking to walk by faith in this world until he comes again.

As we read a particular letter, we can expect that certain passages will immediately grip our heart—giving us some new insight about our Lord or a deepening conviction of how we need to mature in our walk with God. Such discoveries are exciting, and they draw us deeper into God's word to mine its riches. And the best part of studying an entire book is that we can begin to understand our favorite passages in light of the whole letter, which enables us to build a rich, multidimensional understanding of Christ and of the whole Christian life.

We all know how to read a letter: Open the mailbox, see whom the envelope is addressed to, look at the return address, tear it open, sit down with a cup of tea, and enjoy it. The biblical epistles aren't all that different. If we gather a few basic facts about the letter's origin and recipients, and are willing to spend some time savoring its contents, we'll be on the right track. In order to understand the Epistles and rightly apply their messages to our lives, we must take into account three things: (1) the situation of the author, (2) the recipients of the letter, and (3) the letter as a whole.

1. *The situation of the author.* Who was the author? Also, when was the author writing, where was he writing from, and why was he writing? Such details are often revealed in the beginning of the letter, but sometimes at the end. Understanding the epistle's author will give you essential background to his letter's language and themes. It's important to mine this information at the very beginning of your study, and the "Big Picture" introduction (p. xv) will help you to get started.

2. *The recipients of the letter.* Was the author writing to the Jews, God's family from the days of Abraham? Or was the letter addressed to Gentiles, those brought into God's family through faith in Christ? Some letters are addressed to whole churches, and others are addressed to individuals. A number of the Epistles are called "circular letters," which simply means that they were intended to circulate among groups of believers in more than one place. A circular letter was carried by a courier to the nearest church on the address list, and from there it made its way from church

to church. Keep in mind too that the recipient or recipients of a particular letter had a unique background and understanding of God—a *frame of reference*. This frame of reference matters a lot because it's what guides our understanding of the letter and shapes how we apply it. When we read the Epistles, we are reading letters that were given to us by God for our edification, but they were also originally directed at a specific first-century audience. We're opening other people's mail, and knowing their situation helps us see how the letter speaks to our own.

3. *The letter as a whole.* Think for a minute about the zoom feature for a map on a phone. To figure out where you are going, you tend to zoom in close to see a particular street, trying to home in on your destination, but ultimately this street view makes sense only when you zoom back out to see the bigger picture, the entire area surrounding it. This is what it's like to study an epistle in context. With verse-by-verse commentary, you'll be able to zoom in, but in order to understand the close-up, you have to begin with the big picture. So for the "Big Picture" of this epistle, turn the page.

LYDIA BROWNBACK AND MEGAN HILL

The Big Picture of Ephesians

Why Study Ephesians?

We study Ephesians because it's God's word. Passages like 2 Timothy 3 remind us that "all Scripture" (even its hard-to-understand sections!) "is breathed out by God and profitable for teaching, for reproof, for correction, and for training in righteousness, that the man [or woman] of God may be complete, equipped for every good work" (vv. 16–17). Our task as we read Ephesians is to seek to profit from it as God intended. As we do, we'll find that Ephesians teaches us about how God's work of redemption makes us alive, why the church is so important, and what it means to live in Christ. If you've ever wondered about predestination, the roles of husbands and wives, demons and spiritual warfare, and first-century slavery, Ephesians talks about those too. But, mainly, Ephesians is a book about Christ, written for the church. If you want to love Jesus more, Ephesians is for you.

Who Was Paul?

The apostle Paul is the author of Ephesians. Paul was born "Saul" to a Jewish family from Tarsus in Cilicia, a Roman city in what's now Turkey (Acts 22:3). He was a Roman citizen by birth, which gave him the right to a trial—a privilege he later called on (Acts 16:37–39; 22:25–29; 25:6–12). His parents raised him according to Old Testament law, circumcising him when he was eight days old and teaching him to obey all the Jewish commandments and customs (Phil. 3:5). Eventually, young Saul moved to Jerusalem and was educated by the prominent Pharisee and rabbi Gamaliel (Acts 22:3; see also Acts 5:34). He describes himself as "zealous"— both for God (Acts 22:3) and for the church's destruction (Phil. 3:6). As a young adult, he actively persecuted the church and had a hand in the death of Stephen, the first Christian martyr (Acts 7:58; 22:4–5; Phil. 3:6).

One day, the Lord appeared to Saul and confronted him with his rebellion, framing Saul's persecution of the church as persecution of Christ himself ("Saul, Saul, why are you persecuting me?," Acts 9:4). Through this incident on the Damascus Road and the events that followed (Acts 9:1–31), Saul became an apostle—an eyewitness to the resurrected Christ appointed by Christ himself to instruct the early church and write the New Testament Scriptures. Soon, Saul was called Paul (Acts 13:9), and the church sent him out to do the work of a church planter and evangelist throughout the known world, and especially to the Gentiles (Acts 13:1–14:28; 15:35–18:22; 18:22–21:17). During his ministry, Paul wrote almost half of the New Testament (Romans, 1 and 2 Corinthians, Galatians, Ephesians, Philippians, Colossians, 1 and 2 Thessalonians, 1 and 2 Timothy, Titus, and Philemon). He was eventually imprisoned in Rome, having been sent there to appeal the charges against him for preaching the gospel (Acts 28:11–31). This is likely where he died.

As we turn to Ephesians, Paul's biography deepens our appreciation for his epistle. The "Hebrew of Hebrews" (Phil. 3:5) became the apostle to the Gentiles (Eph. 3:1, 8) and proclaimed that Christ reconciles both Jews and Gentiles "in one body through the cross" (2:16). The "persecutor of the church" (Phil. 3:6) later praised the "manifold wisdom of God" revealed in the church (Eph. 3:10). The Roman citizen in chains called himself "a prisoner of Christ Jesus on behalf of you Gentiles" (3:1). Paul's first lesson from Christ— "Saul, Saul, why are you persecuting me?" (Acts 9:4)—became the lesson of Ephesians: The church is "[Christ's] body, the fullness of him who fills all in all" (Eph. 1:23).

One note about Paul's authorship: Since the nineteenth century, progressive scholars have commonly questioned the authorship of various biblical books. Ephesians is no exception. Some argue Paul didn't write Ephesians because Ephesians contains vocabulary and emphasizes theological themes that Paul doesn't include in his other letters. Some also point out that Ephesians is less personal than Paul's other letters (it doesn't mention the names of specific members of the congregation, for example), and so they assert Paul must not be its author. We can't exhaustively counter all those claims here, but it's worth noting that the text of Ephesians plainly says the letter comes from Paul (1:1), and for eighteen centuries Christians universally accepted that. Simply because Paul uses different words, explores different themes, or takes a different tone than he does in other letters doesn't mean he didn't write this one. We can each think of examples from our own lives where we expressed ourselves differently in one situation than we did in another!

Setting of Ephesians

Paul wrote Ephesians between AD 60 and 62, during his Roman imprisonment (see 3:1; 4:1; 6:20). Ephesus was a large port city in Asia, in what is now Turkey, and Paul stayed there for three years (from AD 52 to 55), during his third missionary journey (Acts 19). In the first century, Ephesus was the capital of that region of the Roman Empire, known for its magic arts (Acts 19:19) and its temple to the Greek goddess Artemis (Acts 19:27–28). During Paul's time there, he preached publicly every day as well as performed signs and miracles (Acts 19:8–12). As a result of his ministry, new believers gathered as a church. This letter was penned nearly a decade after he last saw the Ephesian believers in person (Acts 20:38). Nevertheless, he writes, "I do not cease to give thanks for you, remembering you in my prayers" (Eph. 1:16). He may have been far from Ephesus, but the Ephesians were still close to his heart.

Many scholars believe Ephesians, like some of Paul's other letters, was a circular letter, intended to be read by several churches in the area (see Col. 4:16; 1 Thess. 5:27). If so, this may explain the lack of personal greetings and specific references in the letter. Whether or not it was circular in the first century, it's circular now. The letter that the Ephesians read and likely passed along to other congregations now comes in turn to us, thousands of years later, to equip us exactly as it did them—in the knowledge of Christ and in love for his church.

Themes in Ephesians

Ephesians breaks neatly into two related halves. The first half (chaps. 1–3) is more theological and doctrinal, focusing on God's work in believers and the blessings he gives them in Christ. At the time of Paul's writing, the Ephesian church was about ten years old, not brand new but still new enough to be figuring out what it means to be the people of God in a godless world. What's more, the congregation was made up of both Jewish and Gentile converts who needed to understand and live out their fundamental unity together in Christ. In this part of his letter, Paul explores themes including believers' spiritual inheritance, the mystery of the gospel, and the nature of the church.

The second half of Ephesians (chaps. 4–6) is more practical, applying the truths of the letter's first half to believers' new life in Christ. Paul instructs his readers to love and serve one another in the church, home, and workplace; and he equips them for the reality of spiritual warfare. The congregation at Ephesus displayed genuine faith ("your faith in the Lord Jesus," 1:15) and mutual love ("your love toward all the saints," 1:15), but, like all of us, they still had plenty of room to grow. In this part of Ephesians, Paul explores themes including imitating God, submitting to one another, and resisting sin and Satan.

Ephesians for You

If you're a Christian, I hope you belong to a local church that proclaims the gospel. And if you do, I bet you also know that life in the church can sometimes be difficult. You may struggle to get along with believers who seem radically different from you. You may also find it hard to overcome your own sin and weakness in order to serve others. In a variety of ways, congregational life has its challenges. In Ephesians, Paul helps us embrace life together in the church—and he does this in what might seem like a surprising way. Instead of proposing bullet-point strategies to improve body life, he turns our minds and hearts to the body's head: Christ. He shows us how Christ has loved—and continues to love!—the church, and he allows those glorious truths to encourage us to love the church too. I trust that after you finish studying Ephesians, you'll have a greater delight in your local congregation. And if you do, it will be because you have a greater delight in her Savior and Lord.

Outline of Ephesians

1. Greeting (1:1–14)
2. Prayer of thanksgiving (1:15–23)
3. Salvation by grace through faith (2:1–10)
4. Unity and the peace of Christ (2:11–22)
5. Revelation of the gospel mystery (3:1–13)
6. Prayer for strength and insight (3:14–21)
7. Unity of the body of Christ (4:1–16)
8. Paul's testimony (4:17–24)
9. Encouragement for a holy lifestyle (4:25–32)
10. New life in love (5:1–20)
11. Submission to one another (5:21–6:9)
12. The whole armor of God (6:10–20)
13. Conclusion (6:21–24)[1]

---

1 Adapted from "Outline" of Ephesians, in *ESV Concise Study Bible*, ed. Paul R. House et al. (Crossway, 2021), 1308.

Ephesians 1

Blessings in Christ

¹ Paul, an apostle of Christ Jesus by the will of God,

To the saints who are in Ephesus, and are faithful in Christ Jesus:

² Grace to you and peace from God our Father and the Lord Jesus Christ.

Thirteen New Testament books all begin with the same word: "Paul." From Romans to Philemon, readers immediately know they're opening a letter from the Bible's most prolific apostle. Unlike a letter or email that you might receive today, letters in the first century began with the sender's name. The first word of Ephesians tells us that this epistle (letter) was written by Paul, the onetime persecutor turned apostle.

By calling himself an "apostle of Christ Jesus by the will of God," Paul does several things. First, he establishes exactly who he is. Even more importantly, he establishes the authority by which he writes. This isn't just a letter from a friend, a fellow

Christian, a missionary, or a pastor—though it is all those things. It's a letter from an apostle, one of the men appointed by God to lay the church's foundations and proclaim the gospel with authority. Notice that Paul says he's an apostle "by the will of God." From the very beginning of the letter, Paul makes it clear that what he's going to write isn't his own opinions; nor is it important because of his own intellect. God made Paul an apostle, and God gave him the words to write. This, in turn, directs us how to read. We can accept this letter as true, trustworthy, and authoritative, which means we'll try to understand it, apply it to our lives, and submit to it (even when it says things we find hard!). It also means we'll seek God's help, by his Spirit, to do this well. This letter was written down by Paul, but it comes from God—and who better to help us read God's word than God himself?

Paul goes on to identify the first audience of his letter: "the saints who are in Ephesus." As we saw in the introduction (p. xvii), Ephesus was a large port city in Asia. Paul stayed in Ephesus for more than two years on his third missionary journey (Acts 19; 20:17–38). He preached daily in the Hall of Tyrannus to so many people that Acts records "all the residents of Asia heard the word of the Lord" (19:10). As a result, many trusted in Christ and formed a church. It's to that church that Paul wrote this letter.

He writes to "the saints": the holy, set-apart people of God. Although we might be tempted to think of saints as especially godly people who stand out from the rest of us ordinary Christians, Paul calls all the believers in the congregation "saints." He's not denying that they still sin, but he's saying that at the moment of their salvation their fundamental relationship to sin changed. Because of Christ's work on the cross, believers aren't slaves to sin anymore. All who trust in Christ have been set free from sin's penalty and power and have been given Christ's own righteousness. At the moment of salvation, God makes his people holy. Therefore, the Ephesian believers—and all the believers in your own church—are saints.

And these saints were "in Ephesus." The city of Ephesus was the location where these believers lived out their new life, just as your neighborhood or city is the place where you do. The primary descriptor, though, is that they were set apart to belong to God and live faithful lives "in Christ Jesus." Their civic identity was secondary to their spiritual identity. They weren't ordinary citizens of Ephesus. They were in Christ. This identity brought them into a relationship with all "the saints"—everyone else who was likewise in Christ. For us, too, our primary identity lies in our relationship to Christ. And if we're in Christ, we have far more in common with the believers in our church and in churches on the other side of the world than we do with many of the people in our own neighborhoods.

When Paul greets the letter's recipients, he does it with their identity in mind. His greeting is no generic "hello." Because he's writing to "the saints," he extends a spiritual greeting that only saints can receive. "Grace" and "peace" belong exclusively to the people on whom God has poured out his grace and for whom Christ on the cross has secured peace. Although unbelievers may experience what we call God's *common* grace—his giving them food and health and shelter and also relationships and joy, even though they don't acknowledge him—only believers receive his *saving* grace. Only those who are "in Christ" know God's special favor and love. Only those who are "in Christ" can call God "our Father." On the cross, Christ died for his people: paying the penalty we deserved and bringing us into a right relationship with God. In Christ, we enjoy both grace and peace. Thanks be to God!

³ Blessed be the God and Father of our Lord Jesus Christ, who has blessed us in Christ with every spiritual blessing in the heavenly places,

Paul now blesses the God who blesses us. In the original Greek, verses 3–14 are a single sentence. Paul is so amazed by the gloriousness of salvation that he can't hold himself back or confine himself to simple sentences. The English text makes it easier for us to examine each part of what Paul is saying, but we should remember these twelve verses were originally expressed as one long thought.

In his greeting, Paul identified the Christians in Ephesus as "the saints" (v. 1), and here he continues to write to them as a corporate body. In this verse (and throughout his letter) he uses plural words like "our" and "us" to underscore the church members' connectedness. We also know from other passages that the New Testament Epistles were intended to be read aloud in the local church gathering (Col. 4:16; 1 Thess. 5:27). We might be accustomed to reading the Epistles as if they were a private word for each Christian, but they were originally meant as instruction and encouragement for the whole church together. We can make personal application of their truths to our own hearts and lives—and we should!—but we can't overlook the fact that God intended them to be read and applied by whole congregations. As we'll see, Ephesians especially is a book for equipping the church.

The doctrine of the Trinity (the truth that the one God eternally exists as three divine persons: Father, Son, and Holy Spirit) is not always obvious in Scripture. But here we have a clear acknowledgment of God's three-in-one nature. Paul praises God the Father; he affirms our union with the Son, the Lord Jesus; and he describes our blessings as "spiritual"—they come to us by the Spirit. This verse also highlights the way the persons of the Trinity accomplish our redemption. The Father blesses the church, and he blesses us in the Son—it's through Christ's work on the cross and through our union with him by faith that we receive the benefits Paul describes. And the Spirit communicates those blessings to us in the spiritual realm ("the heavenly places").

A final thing to note about this verse is that Paul is stating an accomplished fact. The blessings he's about to describe further are already secured for believers. And he's not describing a limited number of blessings; he says believers have all of them. If you're trusting in Christ for salvation, you've been given every spiritual blessing. At this moment, you have all you need for life in Christ.

EPHESIANS 1:4–6

⁴ even as he chose us in him before the foundation of the world, that we should be holy and blameless before him. In love ⁵ he predestined us for adoption to himself as sons through Jesus Christ, according to the purpose of his will, ⁶ to the praise of his glorious grace, with which he has blessed us in the Beloved.

In these verses, Paul begins to delineate the "spiritual blessing[s] in the heavenly places" (v. 3) that the Ephesian believers possess in Christ. He describes election (the doctrine that God chooses beforehand to save particular people) and adoption (the doctrine that God brings his elect people into relationship with him and makes them part of his family).

Paul's language makes it clear that these blessings—even though they concern human salvation—have God at their center. *God* is the one who chose us in eternity past. Standing blameless before *God* is the point of our being made holy. Being predestined to join *God's* family is the context of our adoption. Our salvation and adoption are accomplished according to *God's* perfect will, and this results in praise to *God* alone.

Paul also emphasizes that our salvation is only "in" and "through" Christ. As Jesus himself proclaimed: "No one comes to the Father except through me" (John 14:6). There's no way to be saved apart from God's becoming man and dying on the cross in our place to bring us into a saving relationship with himself. And Paul puts all this in the context of love. We're predestined to belong to God because of his love. We aren't especially lovable (let's be honest!), but our God is extraordinarily loving. "In love," he sent Christ, "the Beloved," to bless us. Whatever else we may learn from these verses, we should rejoice in this: Our salvation is the work of a loving God.

At this point, you may have some reservations about the doctrine of election. You may wonder how the truth that God chooses people for salvation can be consistent with the fact that you had an experience of deciding to follow God (*Didn't I choose to trust Christ for my salvation?*). Maybe you're also concerned that saying God chooses some will put a damper on evangelism (*Why should I share the gospel if God's already decided who will believe?*) or that it makes God unjust (*If people don't get to choose, is it fair for them to go to hell?*).

Stacks of books have been written on this doctrine, and we can't unpack all the discussions here, but we can affirm a few helpful things. First, the Bible teaches election. It's not an invention of human scholars or theologians. It's clearly stated by God in his word (in these verses and other places too). For this reason, we can't simply dismiss election if it doesn't make sense to us. Instead, we accept it as true and ask God to help us understand it better. Second, the Bible also teaches that people must put their faith in Christ to be saved. In the book of Acts, the jailer asked Paul and Silas, "'Sirs, what must I do to be saved?' And they said, 'Believe in the Lord Jesus, and you will be saved, you and your household'" (Acts 16:30–31). Like the cries of a newborn, trusting in Christ is the vital sign that we've been made alive by God's saving work in our hearts. And if we're alive, these verses assure us that it's because God has loved and chosen us from eternity past. As the old hymn says, "I sought the Lord, and afterward I knew, he moved my soul to seek him seeking me."[1] Third, the Bible teaches us to tell others about the good news of Christ. "Repent and believe in the gospel" (Mark 1:15) was Jesus's sermon to the lost, and it's our message too. We don't know whom God might save, but we do know he's told us to invite everyone to trust in him.

Ultimately, keeping in mind the focus of verses 4–6 helps us delight in the doctrine of election. Salvation is *God's* work—from beginning to end. We don't save ourselves; God saves us. And even when we can't quite reconcile all the implications of election in our own minds, we can humbly rejoice in this truth: Salvation belongs to God. He's in charge, not us. He knows

---

1 Anonymous, "I Sought the Lord and Afterward I Knew," 1878, in *Trinity Hymnal*, rev. ed. (Great Commission, 1990), 466.

what's best; we don't. Confronted with hard questions of judgment and mercy, we can say in faith what Abraham said: "Shall not the Judge of all the earth do what is just?" (Gen. 18:25). And we can add our thanksgiving to what Paul calls "the praise of his glorious grace"!

One more thing: In these verses, Paul uses the word "sons" to describe the people whom God has adopted. It might seem strange as women to think of being "sons." It might even seem like the Bible is discounting the place of women in God's family. (It's not.) To understand why Paul uses this language, remember that Jesus is the Son who has an eternal relationship with the Father. And, as Paul notes, our adoption is through Jesus. When Paul calls us "sons," he's underscoring the fact that we're united to *the* Son. In God's family, we share Christ's position. Even as females, we're sons because our Savior is the Son.[2] There's no better status we could have!

EPHESIANS 1:7–10

[7] In him we have redemption through his blood, the forgiveness of our trespasses, according to the riches of his grace, [8] which he lavished upon us, in all wisdom and insight [9] making known to us the mystery of his will, according to his purpose, which he set forth in Christ [10] as a plan for the fullness of time, to unite all things in Christ, things in heaven and things on earth.

Continuing his praise to God for the spiritual blessings he's given us, Paul now turns to redemption (the doctrine that God rescues

2   Robert Letham, *Union with Christ: In Scripture, History, and Theology* (P&R, 2011), 54n19.

us from slavery to sin and Satan and forgives us through the work of Christ on the cross). He concludes these verses by looking ahead to the ultimate goal of our redemption in eternity future.

When we think about praising God for our salvation, it's probably redemption that we most often have in our minds. To "redeem" something is, of course, to buy it or to buy it back. Paul here uses a word that was commonly used for ransoming slaves.[3] In our redemption, Christ paid the price of our sins and took the condemnation we deserved by his death on the cross. He redeemed us from our slavery to sin and Satan, paid the penalty we owed, and secured the forgiveness of our sins. Paul uses exuberant language like "the riches of his grace . . . lavished upon us." At the cross, Christ accomplished the best thing we could ever hope for: pardon and peace. It's no wonder that redemption is the frequent theme of our hymns and the common focus of our praise to God!

Finally, Paul reveals the future culmination of God's salvation plan: the unity of "all things" under Christ's authority. This unity has been God's purpose all along, but in the Old Testament it was a mystery that was somewhat hidden. Prior to the coming of Christ, believers had only shadows and pictures to point to what God intended to do through his Messiah. But, now, in the time after Christ's death on the cross and establishment of his church, the mystery has been made known to us. In electing, adopting, and redeeming his people throughout history, God is executing his eternal plan to gather a people (the church!) under Christ. His purpose is to make them perfect and whole and then set them in a renewed creation to live together with him forever.

---

3   John R. W. Stott, *The Message of Ephesians: God's New Society*, The Bible Speaks Today, ed. John R. W. Stott (InterVarsity Press, 1979), 40.

If you spend much time following the news, you can be quickly overwhelmed. War breaking out in that country. Political upheaval in this country. Famine over here. Genocide over there. Every part of the world seems to be experiencing some kind of turmoil. The hope of verses 9 and 10 is that human history has a clear trajectory—and it's toward a goal already determined by God himself. In "the fullness of time," every person for whom Christ died will be saved, and Christ's authority over his church and his creation will be put on display for all to see. Right now, the world looks like a mess, but one day God's purposes will be fully accomplished. And on that day, we will give him all glory.

EPHESIANS 1:11–14

11 In him we have obtained an inheritance, having been predestined according to the purpose of him who works all things according to the counsel of his will, **12** so that we who were the first to hope in Christ might be to the praise of his glory. **13** In him you also, when you heard the word of truth, the gospel of your salvation, and believed in him, were sealed with the promised Holy Spirit, **14** who is the guarantee of our inheritance until we acquire possession of it, to the praise of his glory.

Since the beginning of chapter 1, Paul has acted like a kid in a toy store. No sooner has one amazing object caught his attention than a different item on another shelf calls to him. He's dashed up and down the aisles, exclaiming *wow!* over everything he notices. We've already watched him pick up and marvel at the spiritual blessings of election, adoption, redemption, forgiveness, and the future promise of unity under Christ. In verses 11–14, he comes face to face with the final treasure on the highest shelf: our inheritance. Right now—and even more fully in the future—abundant life in God's kingdom is ours.

This might sound too good to be true: an eternity united to Christ, our Savior, clothed in his righteousness; a blessed future with no more sorrow or sin or death; and an unending life of fellowship with God himself. If a stranger promised you this kind of inheritance, you'd laugh him off as a fabulist or a scammer. Even if your loving grandparents or parents offered you these things, you'd rightly be skeptical of their ability to deliver. But Paul shows us that our spiritual inheritance is far more certain than any human-guaranteed inheritance. He traces the source of our inheritance to someone entirely trustworthy and immensely powerful. Our inheritance is assured because *God* predestined it, and he's able to accomplish all his purposes. Everything God wills, he does. From the movement of the tiniest atomic particles to the sustaining of the entire universe, God "works all things according to the counsel of his will." And if he superintends "all things," then our inheritance in Jesus Christ is also safely in his hands.

If that weren't enough, he also gives us a guarantee: "the promised Holy Spirit." When you want to purchase a house or car, the bank will ask you for a substantial amount of money as the surety that you'll follow through with the sale. They hold that money until you come up with the rest of the purchase price. In the same way (even though he is under no obligation to do so!), the Lord gives us his Spirit as security that we will one day possess eternal life in his kingdom. Do you have the indwelling Spirit? Well, then you can be sure you'll also have the inheritance.

Our full inheritance will be ours in the future, but even now we live confidently in new spiritual life. Christians are those who "hope in Christ." While people might commonly use the word "hope" to express something like a wish or a desire—*I hope this recipe turns out okay* or *I hope I get that job I applied for*—the Bible uses "hope" to mean something unseen but nevertheless certain (see Heb. 10:23). If we "hope in Christ" we set our hearts on him "to the praise of his glory." In this life and the life to come, Christ is all our joy, all our praise, all our expectation. As the hymnwriter Elizabeth Payson Prentiss wrote,

> Once earthly joy I craved,
> Sought peace and rest;
> Now Thee alone I seek,
> Give what is best;
> This all my prayer shall be:
> More love, O Christ, to Thee,
> More love to Thee,
> More love to Thee![4]

Finally, Paul's "we" and "us" language in this section affirms that these spiritual blessings belong equally to both Jews and Gentiles, a theme he'll develop further in chapter 2. The Jews were "the first" to believe; they recognized Jesus as the long-promised Messiah of Old Testament prophecy. But the Gentiles, too, received salvation. When they heard the gospel, they believed and received the Holy Spirit. The Spirit was "promised" to them, which affirms that their inclusion among God's people wasn't an afterthought but was God's purpose all along. And both Jews and Gentiles have a share in the spiritual inheritance God is keeping for them. No

---

4 Elizabeth Payson Prentiss, "More Love to Thee, O Christ," 1856, in *Trinity Hymnal*, rev. ed. (Great Commission, 1990), 649.

matter a person's ethnicity or religious upbringing, her salvation is "to the praise of [God's] glory."

15 For this reason, because I have heard of your faith in the Lord Jesus and your love toward all the saints, **16** I do not cease to give thanks for you, remembering you in my prayers, **17** that the God of our Lord Jesus Christ, the Father of glory, may give you the Spirit of wisdom and of revelation in the knowledge of him,

Isn't it great to get good news from friends? When you go to the mailbox and find a birth announcement, a wedding invitation, a Christmas card, or—rarest of all in this online age—a letter, your heart swells a bit, doesn't it? It's wonderful to hear that someone you love is doing well. In these verses, Paul says he had received a good report about the Ephesian congregation, and his response to this joyful news is to bow in prayer. Beginning in verse 15, chapter 1 contains Paul's prayer for the Ephesians. In verses 15–17, he explains the circumstances of his prayer and then sets up the main petition of his prayer: that God would give the Ephesians deeper knowledge of himself.

Paul prayed because he was invested in the Ephesians' spiritual well-being. While it's perfectly appropriate to rejoice in news of someone's new house or new baby, the news that here moved Paul to joyful thanksgiving was the report that the believers were flourishing spiritually. We can learn something from Paul's interest in his friends' souls. We shouldn't be concerned only about our fellow Christians' health or jobs; we should be concerned ultimately about whether they're persisting in their faith and whether they're demonstrating it by loving other believers.

Paul also models mature prayer habits. His prayer for the Ephesians is persistent, thankful, and deliberate. First, he says he does "not cease" to pray for them. Day after day (probably even "night and day," 1 Thess. 3:10), he brings the Ephesians before the throne of God. Next, his prayer is filled with thanksgiving. Paul knows the Ephesians' spiritual well-being isn't ultimately the Ephesians' doing. *God* had given the Ephesians the gift of faith and love, and so Paul thanks him. Finally, Paul's prayer is intentional: He "remember[s]" the Ephesians. No matter what else was on his list for the day, Paul didn't let prayer for the Ephesians slip his mind. In these verses, Paul shows us that he practices what he preaches, living out his own exhortation from 1 Thessalonians: "Rejoice always, pray without ceasing, give thanks in all circumstances; for this is the will of God in Christ Jesus for you" (5:16–18).

In the first half of the chapter, Paul introduced his doxology of praise with the three persons of the Trinity (Eph. 1:3), now he frames his prayer for the Ephesians with the Trinity (v. 17). Paul prays to "the Father of glory." Similarly, when Jesus taught his disciples—and us!—to pray, he taught us to pray to "our Father in heaven" (Matt. 6:9). Second, Paul prays in relationship to the Son. It's only those who have a relationship with Christ, who can call him "*our* Lord Jesus Christ," who can claim the privilege of prayer.[5] By his death on the cross, Christ reconciled us to God and so secured our right to talk to God. Even now, Christ is at the Father's right hand, interceding for us as we pray (Rom. 8:34; see also Heb. 7:25). Third, Paul asks for the Spirit. The Ephesians already had the Spirit

---

5   "Q. What is prayer? A. Prayer is an offering up of our desires unto God for things agreeable to his will, in the name of Christ, with confession of our sins, thankful acknowledgement of his mercies." Westminster Shorter Catechism, in *The Westminster Confession of Faith: Together with the Larger Catechism and the Shorter Catechism with Scripture Proofs*, 3rd ed. (Christian Education and Publications, 1990), 98.

dwelling in them from the moment of their new birth. But they were also always in need of the Spirit. Paul's request reminds us of Jesus's teaching on prayer: "If you then, who are evil, know how to give good gifts to your children, how much more will the heavenly Father give the Holy Spirit to those who ask him!" (Luke 11:13). Whatever we may ask from God, the Spirit is the ultimate fulfillment of all our needs and desires. When we pray for our friends, we should model Paul's prayer and ask God to give them his Spirit. Are they deciding about a job? Ask God to give them the wisdom that comes from his Spirit (Eph. 1:17; Col. 1:9). Are they fighting sin? Ask God to send his Spirit to lead them in righteousness (Rom. 14:17). Are they sick or lonely or discouraged? Ask God to give them the Spirit's comfort (Acts 9:31). When we ask God to give us his Spirit, we ask him to give us himself. As the early American theologian Jonathan Edwards explained, "God himself is the great good desired and sought after."[6] What more could we ask?

Finally, Paul declares the main point of his request for the Ephesians: "revelation in the knowledge of him." This might seem like an unhelpfully simple prayer. With all the Ephesians had going on, Paul wants them to just know God? Don't they already know God?

We should understand that "knowledge" is both head knowledge and lived experience—and both are important. On the one hand, Paul wants the Ephesians to fill their minds with who God is and what he has done for them in Christ. Some of us may be tempted to discount the spiritual importance of learning information about God, but Jesus says truth is essential to worship: "The true worshipers will worship the Father in spirit and truth, for the Father is seeking such

---

6   Jonathan Edwards, *An Humble Attempt*, in *The Works of Jonathan Edwards*, vol. 5, *Apocalyptic Writings*, ed. Stephen J. Stein, WJE Online, accessed December 10, 2024, http://edwards .yale.edu/.

people to worship him" (John 4:23). Deep knowledge about God moves us to deep worship of God. Paul also wants the Ephesians to have what the Puritans would call "experiential" knowledge of God. He wants them to know him the way you know your parents or your siblings—you know lots of facts about them, sure, but you also know them because you've lived with them and you love them. We may be tempted to dismiss the importance of this type of knowledge, too. When we simply want others to believe God is real or to affirm that Jesus died on the cross, we aim too low. We ought to want what Paul wants: head knowledge about God *and* heart experience of God.

But didn't the Ephesians already have this knowledge? Yes and no. Paul's prayer echoes the words of the psalmist:

One thing have I asked of the LORD,
    that I will seek after:
that I may dwell in the house of the LORD
    all the days of my life,
to gaze upon the beauty of the LORD
    and to inquire in his temple. (Ps. 27:4)

Believers who know God should always want to know him more, to be where he is, to meditate on his loveliness. We can never have enough of God. And as the next verses of Paul's prayer will show us, God has depths that will take an eternity to discover.

EPHESIANS 1:18–21

¹⁸ having the eyes of your hearts enlightened, that you may know what is the hope to which he has called you, what are the riches of his glorious inheritance in the saints, ¹⁹ and what is the immea-

surable greatness of his power toward us who believe, according to the working of his great might **20** that he worked in Christ when he raised him from the dead and seated him at his right hand in the heavenly places, **21** far above all rule and authority and power and dominion, and above every name that is named, not only in this age but also in the one to come.

Paul now prays for God to grant the Ephesians three areas of knowledge: the hope of God's calling, the riches of God's inheritance, and the greatness of God's power toward them. These are spiritual truths, and it requires spiritual eyes ("the eyes of your hearts") to appreciate them. As we saw in Paul's earlier doxology of praise, the beginning and end of our new spiritual life is God. Our salvation reveals truths about ourselves and truths about salvation's benefits, but its ultimate lesson is about our glorious Lord.

The first way Paul wants the Ephesians to grow in their knowledge of God is by understanding the hope of their calling. Remember, throughout this prayer, he has in view both head knowledge and heart knowledge. The Ephesians need to be sure of the facts of their calling, and they need to experience the hope that their calling gives. A believer's calling is the invitation from God to follow Christ. Unlike a human invitation to a party or a concert, which invitees may either accept or decline, God's calling is *effectual*: The people he calls will come to him (see John 6:37). The first disciples abandoned nets and boats to orient their lives around Jesus (Luke 5:1–11); similarly, all those whom God calls step into a completely new life and don't look back. Believers love, obey, trust, worship, enjoy, and serve Christ in everything. As they do, they look ahead to an eternal future where they will see Christ face to face and live with him forever. Compared to the futility and meaninglessness of life apart from Christ, the called life is deeply hopeful.

Believers also grow in their knowledge of God by meditating on the riches of God's inheritance. Commentators are divided about whether "his glorious inheritance in the saints" in this text is the spiritual inheritance that believers receive or the believers as the inheritance that God receives. We find both ideas in Scripture. God does store up spiritual blessings for his people (see Col. 1:12, for example), and the blessing of our salvation is a kind of inheritance that God gives us (as we saw in Eph. 1:11 and 14). But it seems more likely that this verse is talking about believers as God's inheritance. Notably, Paul calls it "his" inheritance, which indicates that the saints are a glorious treasure belonging to God.

If you look around at the members of your church, "glorious" might not be the first word that comes to mind. But the work of Christ testifies to their true value. God's people could be purchased at no smaller price than God's blood (Acts 20:28). Elsewhere, Peter invites believers to meditate on their status as God's priceless possession: "But you are a chosen race, a royal priesthood, a holy nation, a people for his own possession, that you may proclaim the excellencies of him who called you out of darkness into his marvelous light" (1 Pet. 2:9). Knowing that God set us apart for his own leads us to worship.

Paul identifies a third area of knowledge he desires for the Ephesians: "the immeasurable greatness of [God's] power" (Eph. 1:19). Paul presents Jesus's resurrection, ascension, and heavenly reign as exhibits of God's might. Jesus was dead, but God made him alive. God raised him to the heavenly places, gave him authority over all things, and exalted him above every earthly and spiritual power. Christ's reign may be invisible now ("in this age"), but it is no less real. And one day soon, his reign will be revealed ("in the [age] to come") for all to see (see also Phil. 2:9–11).

Again, Paul wants the Ephesians to know this truth in both their minds and hearts. God accomplished these acts in Christ by his "great might," and by this same power he works in his people. From Acts 19, we know that the believers in Ephesus were highly interested in the subject of power. Prior to their conversion, many of them had practiced magic arts, investing heavily in books purporting to give them spiritual powers (Acts 19:18–20). But the power of Christ is a different kind of power altogether. Rather than causing bondage and harm like the evil spirits of Ephesus did, the Lord gives life and peace. The one who raised the Son and established him in heaven will one day raise us and establish us alongside him (Eph. 2:5–7). In this life, God is mightily working all things for his glory and our good (Rom. 8:28–29). His power is "toward us who believe."

EPHESIANS 1:22–23

²² And he put all things under his feet and gave him as head over all things to the church, ²³ which is his body, the fullness of him who fills all in all.

If you could have authority over one thing, what would you choose? Maybe you'd want to be the CEO at your workplace and steer your company's goals. Maybe you'd like to oversee your neighborhood and finally get those potholes repaired. Maybe you'd even like to be president of the whole country. You'd really be in charge then! If these reflect our aspirations for power, we might expect that Christ's rule would also focus on economies or municipalities or governments. But when verses 22–23 bring us to the pinnacle of Christ's honor and reign, we discover that its ultimate expression is his authority over everything *for the good of the church.*

Paul begins by affirming that Christ rules over the entire universe. God put "all things under his feet." Not a bird or boulder is outside his command. Markets and nations and sea levels rise and fall at his direction. And he is "head over all things *to the church.*" Every turning point of human history, every crop harvest, and every scientific advance is orchestrated by him for the ultimate good of his people. By these things, he provides for his people, and he sends out the gospel to expand his kingdom. Although Christ is Lord of all creation, his rule in the world is largely unnoticed. Our unbelieving neighbors don't acknowledge that God directs their paths for the sake of the church. National governments don't believe their foreign policy is designed by God to advance his kingdom. Believers, however, know the truth. Christ is the head of all things, and he turns the whole world for the church's good.

Christ also rules *in* the church, and he rules it intimately. In the church, we openly proclaim him as King and willingly bow under his command. His word is our law, and his honor is our glory. The church "is his body." Nothing else in creation is described this way. Only the people God has redeemed by Christ's blood and gathered as a community of worshipers are so connected to Christ as to be his body. It's obvious to all of us that a body can't survive without a head. To be brain-dead is to be unable to function; each organ and process needs the head to prompt and animate it. Likewise, the church and Christ are intimately joined. Without Christ, the head, the church-body could not live. Passages like 1 Corinthians 12 teach us that Christ gives the Spirit to his church (vv. 4–11). Christ gives gifts to his church (vv. 8–11, 27–31).

Christ gives unity to his church (vv. 4–6, 12–13, 25–26). Christ gives purpose to his church (v. 7). Christ equips the church for ministry (vv. 4–11, 28–31). Christ even gives the members to the church (v. 18). Paul first learned the lesson of Christ's inseparable connection to his church at the moment of his conversion. When Christ appeared to Saul as he was heading out to harm the church, the Lord impressed on him that to attack the church was to attack Christ himself: "Saul, Saul, why are you persecuting me?" (Acts 9:4). How we view and treat the church is how we view and treat Christ. The church is his body.

Finally, Paul describes the church with a somewhat puzzling phrase: "the fullness of him who fills all in all" (Eph. 1:23). Paul seems to be saying both that Christ fills his church and that the church is the fullness of Christ.[7] We experience Christ filling his church when the members are gathered together and each one uses her gifts for the good of the whole. Each member has a measure of the Spirit, but Christ has the Spirit "without measure" (John 3:34; see also Rom. 12:3). We each have some gifts, but Christ has all the gifts. In the church—where all the parts of the body are brought together—we can experience the fullness of Christ who fills us. When you look around your local congregation and see a variety of gifts and graces at work, you glimpse the breadth of Christ himself. Paul also says that the church is "the fullness of [Christ]" (Eph. 1:23). A head isn't a head without a body; a king isn't a king without a kingdom; a redeemer isn't a redeemer without a people. The very existence of the church affirms the glory of Christ. As the people of God worship and work together, we display Christ himself.

---

7 Matthew Henry, *Matthew Henry's Commentary*, vol. 6, *Acts to Revelation* (1710; repr., Hendrickson, 1991), 556.

Ephesians is a book about Christ and for the church (as we'll see in the coming chapters), so it's fitting that Paul ends his opening prayer for the Ephesians with the glorious reality of Christ's lordship over his church. Christ fills the church with his fullness, and the church is the fullness of Christ. There's no better place to be.

Ephesians 2

Salvation and Unity

¹ And you were dead in the trespasses and sins ² in which you once walked, following the course of this world, following the prince of the power of the air, the spirit that is now at work in the sons of disobedience— ³ among whom we all once lived in the passions of our flesh, carrying out the desires of the flesh and the mind, and were by nature children of wrath, like the rest of mankind.

Nobody likes to dwell on the sins and failings of her past. After you've become a Christian, it can be uncomfortable to think about aspects of your former life. And yet, that's exactly what Paul does here. In these three verses, he takes a long, hard look at the Ephesians' past, before they trusted in Christ and received new life in him. As we'll see, it's not pretty.

First, Paul says that the believers were once "dead." It doesn't get much worse than that! Scripture's consistent testimony is that people who are apart from Christ are not merely sick or sluggish but spiritually dead. A dead person, of course, can do nothing to help herself. So, too, a spiritually dead person is powerless to improve her condition. She can't make herself alive; she can't even ask someone else for assistance. The reason for this deadness is "trespasses and sins." Those two words sum up the wickedness that cuts unbelievers off from life in Christ. "Trespasses" refers to rebellion against God's law; "sin" refers to failure to live up to God's righteous standard.[1] Once upon a time, the evil things we did and the good things we failed to do were a symptom of our spiritual death.

As you think back on your life as an unbeliever—or as you look at the unbelievers around you today—it might not seem like unbelievers are "dead" or that their lives are characterized by "trespasses and sins." Your social media feed is probably filled with "dead" people who are running marathons, creating art, helping their communities, and caring for their children. But these verses tell us that even when unbelievers are physically alive and doing good things, their souls lack the spiritual life that comes only through Christ.

Second, Paul reveals the authorities the Ephesians once obeyed. He says they followed "the course of this world." In Scripture, the "world" doesn't usually refer to planet Earth; it refers to the realm of those who reject God and his gospel. Paul is saying that, as unbelievers, the Ephesians succumbed to the worst kind of peer pressure. Whatever sin was popular was the sin they took up. He says they also followed "the prince of the power of the air." Elsewhere, this wicked ruler is called an "adversary" and a "roaring lion" (1 Pet. 5:8), a "thief" (John 10:10), and the "dragon, that ancient serpent, who is the devil and Satan" (Rev. 20:2). Unbelievers do

---

1   John R. W. Stott, *The Message of Ephesians: God's New Society*, The Bible Speaks Today (InterVarsity Press, 1979), 71.

the devil's bidding, and the Ephesians, too, once eagerly followed his evil suggestions. Prior to conversion, the Ephesians (and all of us) were also in bondage to our own sinful desires, "the passions of our flesh, carrying out the desires of the flesh and the mind" (Eph. 2:3). In Galatians, Paul lists some of the works of the flesh: "sexual immorality, impurity, sensuality, idolatry, sorcery, enmity, strife, jealousy, fits of anger, rivalries, dissensions, divisions, envy, drunkenness, orgies, and things like these" (5:19–21). As unbelievers, we regularly satisfied ourselves at the expense of others and without regard to God.

Theologians talk about the world, the flesh, and the devil as the three primary influences on our sinful choices, and in these verses we see that evil triumvirate at work. Throughout our preconversion past we were enslaved to those three masters, even if we didn't recognize it. It's one feature of the blinding nature of sin that unbelievers fail to understand their condition and choices. In our world, to be "transgressive" is to be free, to make daring decisions apart from constraints, to boldly push boundaries in new and exciting ways. Unbelievers often think they're doing something courageous, willful, and innovative. But Scripture says they're dead and enslaved followers, jumping to attention whenever one of their masters crooks a finger. When we consider our own past, we realize that we too obeyed sin and Satan with a prompt "Yes, sir!" every time.

Paul's final phrase in this passage describes the universal condition of everyone apart from Christ: "by nature children of wrath, like the rest of mankind." Prior to our salvation, God rightly considered us his enemies and rebels against his holy rule. Every sin deserves God's wrath and curse, and so we were once under God's just judgment. Paul also affirms that we didn't become sinners by doing bad things—we were sinners "by nature," from the very beginning of our existence (see Ps. 51:3–5; Rom. 1:18; 5:12–14). The particular sins we committed were simply expressions of our inherent sinfulness. Finally, these verses reveal that this dead and enslaved condition was true of everyone ("like the rest of mankind"), not just those we might consider especially sinful. This truth puts us on the same level with every believer; before the Spirit worked in us, our situation was grim. The girl who was saved as a three-year-old at vacation Bible school and the woman who was saved last year while in prison have the same testimony. They were once rebels under God's wrath. Paul's words also put us—when we were alienated from Christ—on the same level with unbelievers. Back then, we weren't any better off than our unbelieving neighbors are today. Taking a long look at our past isn't fun, but it helpfully humbles us. We couldn't do anything by our own power. We deserved only God's just judgment. We weren't superior to anyone else. And, as we'll see in the next verses, our only hope was God.

EPHESIANS 2:4–7

⁴ But God, being rich in mercy, because of the great love with which he loved us, ⁵ even when we were dead in our trespasses, made us alive together with Christ—by grace you have been saved— ⁶ and raised us up with him and seated us with him in the heavenly places in Christ Jesus, ⁷ so that in the coming ages he might show the immeasurable riches of his grace in kindness toward us in Christ Jesus.

These verses might be the most beautiful surprise in all Scripture. Having walked us slowly through the underground sewage tunnel of our past, Paul rounds a bend and—hallelujah!—we see light.

These verses make sense of why such unpleasant truths pervaded the previous section. We needed to acknowledge the gloom in order to appreciate the sunrise. Now we can bask in God's grace toward us.

Even just the first two words contain spiritual treasure: "But" brings us up sharply, signaling a radical contrast to the horrors we've just meditated on. This is the plot twist we've been hoping for, the moment our story's protagonist steps in to set everything right. And it turns out "God" is that hero. Without God, our story would have continued its inexorable slide into sin and judgment. *God* is the one who appears; *God* is the one who acts; *God* is the one who saves. God—not us—is the main character in our life's narrative. The rest of this text reveals God's reasons for saving us, the way he saved us, and his ultimate purposes in saving us.

First, we see God's reasons for saving us—and all are rooted in his character. God saved us because he is "rich in mercy." Six times in this letter, Paul uses some form of the word "riches" to describe God's grace, mercy, or glory displayed in Christ (1:7, 18; 2:4, 7; 3:8, 16). He's not just merciful; he's rich in mercy. He is, as he revealed to Moses long ago, "the LORD, the LORD, a God merciful and gracious, slow to anger, and abounding in steadfast love and faithfulness" (Ex. 34:6). God saved us also "because of the great love with which he loved us" (Eph. 2:4). The reason God loves us has nothing to do with us and everything to do with him. While we might rescue a kitten, smile at a toddler, and marry a man because something about them is lovable, God loved us simply because he chose to do so. In fact, he loved us *in spite of* our character ("even when we were dead in our trespasses"). At great cost to himself, and from eternity past, God determined to be good to us and set his affection on us. Nothing we did qualifies us to be loved by God, and so nothing can disqualify us either. This is circular reasoning we can receive with grateful hearts: He loved us because he loved us. And he saved us out of his grace ("by grace you have been saved"). "Grace" is God's favor toward ill-deserving sinners. As we saw in verses 1–3, we were God's enemies, rebels against his law and servants of Satan. But God is gracious. When we deserved his wrath (v. 3), he gave us his salvation. God also saved us out of his "kindness." From beginning to end, all God's ways toward his people are for their good. Truly there is no God like ours!

Paul then goes on to describe how God saved us. The doctrine of salvation is a diamond with many facets, and any one biblical passage doesn't cover them all. In 1:7, for example, Paul highlighted the forgiveness of our sins. In these verses in chapter 2, he focuses on another aspect of salvation: union with Christ. Notice Paul's use of the phrase "with Christ": We were made alive together "with Christ," raised "with him," and seated "with him." Additionally, Paul says we are "in Christ Jesus." The Puritan Thomas Goodwin explained our union with Christ with a helpful illustration: In God's sight, there are only two men, Adam and Jesus Christ, and "these two between them had all the rest of the sons of men hanging at their girdle."[2] Goodwin is saying that all of us were born hanging from Adam's belt. Wherever Adam went, we went too: into sin, into death, into judgment. But, when God saves us, he takes us off Adam's belt and hooks us to Christ's belt. Now, wherever Christ goes, we go too: into obedience, into (and out of!) the grave, into resurrection life, into God's presence in the heavenly places. Christ reverses all the horrible realities of verses 1–3. When we say the Apostles' Creed, we affirm that Christ "rose again from the dead. He ascended into heaven and is seated at the right hand of God the Father."[3] Ephesians 2 teaches

---

2 Thomas Goodwin, *The Works of Thomas Goodwin*, vol. 4 (Edinburgh, 1861), 31.
3 "The Apostles' Creed," in *Trinity Hymnal*, rev. ed. (Great Commission, 1990), 845.

us that what's true of Christ is also true of all who are united to him. In Christ, you died to your sin and receive resurrection life now and a secure future in the life to come.

Finally, Paul shows us the purpose of God's saving work: "so that in the coming ages he might show the immeasurable riches of his grace in kindness toward us in Christ Jesus." God saved us so that in every future age—times to come both in this life and in the next—we will display the riches of his grace. When the members of your church walk around town, and especially when you assemble to worship, you are living evidence that God is merciful, gracious, loving, and kind. What's more, "in the coming ages," when God's people gather in that "great multitude that no one could number . . . standing before the throne and before the Lamb" (Rev. 7:9), our very existence will show the riches of his grace toward us in Christ. Proverbs says, "In a multitude of people is the glory of a king" (14:28), and so it is with our Lord. When we are joined to him through Christ, we swell the ranks of his subjects, and he's exalted as a great king forever.

EPHESIANS 2:8–10

⁸ For by grace you have been saved through faith. And this is not your own doing; it is the gift of God, ⁹ not a result of works, so that no one may boast. ¹⁰ For we are his workmanship, created in Christ Jesus for good works, which God prepared beforehand, that we should walk in them.

From your very first babysitting job, you've known what it means to earn something. You changed dirty diapers, solved sibling squabbles, and made sure the cat didn't escape through the open front door. By the time the parents came home, you'd earned every penny of the twenty-dollar bill they handed you. But what if, instead, you'd spent those hours neglecting the kids, drawing on the walls with a permanent marker, and encouraging the cat to make a run for it? And what if the parents still smiled when they came home and handed you a twenty? That would be pure grace. In these verses, Paul underscores the fact that not only did we not earn our salvation but that we actively rebelled against God, and yet he gave us salvation anyway. Because of that, then, we seek to obey and please him—not to earn our salvation but to express our gratitude for it.

Verses 8 and 9 emphasize the sovereign kindness of God in saving sinners. We have been saved "by grace . . . through faith." "Faith," in Scripture, is never faith in the abstract, in the way our coworkers and neighbors might use the word. Unbelievers propose "having faith" as a kind of positive thinking that can mitigate life's troubles. But "faith," in Scripture, is always faith in a person; it's always faith in the Lord Jesus Christ, crucified and risen for sinners. It's also important to note the connection between grace and faith. Faith itself is an admission that we can do nothing and God must do everything.[4] And even this cry for rescue is beyond the ability of dead sinners. God must put it in our hearts. Nothing about our salvation is our "own doing" or "a result of works." All of it is given to us. This truth prevents us from prideful boasting. As we saw in verses 1–3, prior to our salvation we deserved only God's wrath and were no better off than any other sinner. And as we saw in verses 4–7, God loved

---

4 As the Puritan Thomas Manton said, faith is "the empty hand of the soul . . . [that] looketh for all from God." Thomas Manton, *James*, Geneva Series of Commentaries (1693; repr., Banner of Truth, 1998), 455.

us simply because he loved us, not because we were lovelier than anyone else. Confronted with sin and sinners in this world, the Christian will always acknowledge with genuine gratitude, "There, but for the grace of God, go I."[5]

Having been saved entirely by God's work, we are now given work to do. Paul calls us God's "workmanship"—we ourselves are the product of his work. We are "created" in Christ Jesus—made new by Christ's saving work on our behalf. Who we are today is because of what God has done in us. It's fitting, then, that we should seek to spend our new lives obeying, serving, and pleasing him. We've already seen that we do nothing to earn our salvation, so these "good works" don't contribute to our right standing before God. Instead, they are the works of someone in whom God has already worked. We are no longer slaves to sin and Satan but willing servants of our loving Savior. Like the child whose attempts to sweep the floor are received with smiles and hugs by her mom, our obedience pleases the Father whose love for us is already assured.

What "good works" await you today? As you visit a hospitalized church member, sing hymns with your roommates, pray for your grandchildren, or share the gospel with your coworkers, you are doing something extremely important. Although you may not always feel gifted for the task at hand, you can take confidence that these are exactly the good works for which God created you. And although each day's kingdom to-dos sometimes seem random and insignificant, you can rest in the fact that God selected each one from eternity past for you to walk in. A load of laundry done for an elderly neighbor isn't just a load of laundry. It's the precise task

5   This phrase is attributed to the English Puritan John Bradford, who supposedly said, "There, but for the grace of God, goes John Bradford."

that God made for you and made you for. Encouraged by this, we should seek out good works and do them with joy.

¹¹ Therefore remember that at one time you Gentiles in the flesh, called "the uncircumcision" by what is called the circumcision, which is made in the flesh by hands— ¹² remember that you were at that time separated from Christ, alienated from the commonwealth of Israel and strangers to the covenants of promise, having no hope and without God in the world.

Just when we thought Paul had stopped surveying our unpleasant past, he dives back in for another look. As with verses 1–3, this backward reflection gives us reason for sober humility. Thankfully, Paul's last tour ended with the glorious grace of God in our salvation, and, if we glance ahead, we can see this one will too. But for now, it's good for us to "remember" our previous condition: We were once separated from God and separated from his people.

Gentiles (people who aren't Jewish) were routinely looked down on by Jews in the first century. Jews called Gentiles names ("the uncircumcision") and considered them inferior. The obvious marker of Gentiles was that they hadn't been circumcised—hadn't received the sign "in the flesh" that demonstrated their submission to God's law and inclusion among his people (see Gen. 17:10–14). This was a stark contrast to the circumcised Jews who faithfully presented their boy babies on the eighth day in obedience to God's command. But even though Jews had received circumcision, Paul also points out that their circumcision was "made in the flesh by hands." Both Jews and

Gentiles were missing what really mattered.[6] Gentiles' uncircumcised flesh was a sign of their failure to know and worship the true God. Jews' circumcised flesh was often an excuse for spiritual pride and a merely outward show of piety. What both Jews and Gentiles truly needed was a new, Spirit-filled heart—one that loved and worshiped God above all else. In verse 11, Paul chips away at the division between Gentile and Jew (a theme he'll develop later in chapter 2).

The Gentiles' uncircumcision was a symptom of their even deeper problem. Because they didn't know and submit to God's law, they were "separated from Christ" and "without God in the world." They didn't have God's law—his perfect revelation of his character and will—laid up in their hearts (see Deut. 11:18–19). They were ignorant pagans. Their lack of knowledge of God and lack of obedience to him meant they also lacked his presence with them. The Lord dwelt with his Jewish people (first in the tabernacle and then in the temple), spoke to them by his law and prophets, and bound them to himself by his covenants. Gentiles had none of that. They were without God.

The other implication for Gentiles' ignorant disobedience is that they were cut off from God's people. Paul says they were "alienated from the commonwealth of Israel and strangers to the covenants of promise." Having a relationship with God and having a relationship with God's people are inextricably linked. If you don't honor God, you can't belong to his covenant people. This is true even today. In our churches, when the elders require members to give a credible testimony of faith and new life in Christ, they are maintaining the link between faith and belonging that has always existed. With no such testimony, the Gentiles couldn't enjoy the benefits of being

6   Bryan Chapell, *Ephesians*, Reformed Expository Commentary, ed. Richard D. Phillips and Philip Graham Ryken (P&R, 2009), 95.

part of God's people. They were people without a country. Just as undocumented immigrants don't have the security that comes with citizenship, the Gentiles didn't have a place in Israel's commonwealth and so weren't guaranteed the blessings of God's covenant promises.

Worst of all, they had "no hope." Unlike their Jewish neighbors, the Gentiles weren't looking for the seed of the woman who would crush the head of the serpent (Gen. 3:15). They didn't have the prophecies that foretold the promised Messiah ("Christ"), who would rescue his people (Isa. 9:6–7). They didn't know they could go to the Jews for spiritual light (Zech. 8:22–23). They couldn't anticipate Jesus. The family history of the Ephesians—and of us all today who are Gentiles—was a stunted and shriveled tree. Without God. Without belonging. Without hope.

EPHESIANS 2:13–18

[13] But now in Christ Jesus you who once were far off have been brought near by the blood of Christ. [14] For he himself is our peace, who has made us both one and has broken down in his flesh the dividing wall of hostility [15] by abolishing the law of commandments expressed in ordinances, that he might create in himself one new man in place of the two, so making peace, [16] and might reconcile us both to God in one body through the cross, thereby killing the hostility. [17] And he came and preached peace to you who were far off and peace to those who were near. [18] For through him we both have access in one Spirit to the Father.

If the previous section (vv. 11–12) was a tale of suspense in which the characters were trapped in a dangerous and seemingly inextricable situation and all seemed lost, this section (vv. 13–18) has the power to change everything. "But now," Paul begins, "in Christ Jesus . . ." At last, we can exhale, knowing the story will turn out all right in the end. Having surveyed the grim past of all Gentiles—separated from God and cut off from his people—Paul reveals the new unity that Christ accomplished: Gentiles and Jews in a right relationship with God and one another. As in verse 4, the main character of this story is God. Gentiles and Jews were each powerless to create unity, but "in Christ Jesus" the impossible becomes reality.

In these verses, Paul describes the Gentiles as being "far off" and the Jews as "near." As we saw in verses 11 and 12, the Gentiles were separated from God because they didn't have his word, covenants, promises, or presence. This separated them from God's people too. The Jews, on the other hand, had all the blessings of a relationship with God right in their midst. But in the sending of Christ, God intervened and brought both groups near to him. The blood of Christ on the cross, which makes atonement for sin and reconciles sinners to God, was shed for both Gentiles and Jews. No matter their ethnicity, those who trust in Christ by faith, "through him . . . have access in one Spirit to the Father." (Note: Paul again emphasizes the Trinity!) In Christ, Jewish people have access to the Father by the indwelling Spirit—a nearer relationship to God than they ever before had. In Christ, Gentile people are "brought near" to enjoy the same.

Christ's work on the cross didn't merely accomplish reconciliation between God and man; it also accomplished reconciliation between man and man. Christ makes Jews and Gentiles "one body . . . , thereby killing the hostility." They become united in the church. Christ accomplished this unity in a number of ways. First, Paul says Christ broke down "the dividing wall of hostility." Here, Paul may be alluding to the literal barrier that existed in the first-century temple to separate Jews and Gentiles. The early Jewish historian Josephus described it this way: "A partition made of stone all round, whose height was three cubits . . . upon it stood pillars at equal distance from one another, declaring the law of purity, some in Greek and some in Roman letters, that 'no foreigner shall go within that sanctuary.' "[7] Prior to Christ, when Jews and Gentiles came to worship, they had to go separate ways. But, in Christ, they are freed to worship together "in one body."

Next, Paul says that Christ abolished "the law of commandments expressed in ordinances." Jesus himself said, "Do not think that I have come to abolish the Law or the Prophets; I have not come to abolish them but to fulfill them" (Matt. 5:17), so Paul isn't talking about the continuing moral law (like the Ten Commandments). Instead, he's talking about the Old Testament ceremonial law (like ritual cleansings, circumcision, and the sacrificial system) that created a barrier between observant Jews and nonobservant Gentiles. By doing away with these aspects of Old Testament worship, Christ erased many of the outward divisions between Jew and Gentile.

Finally in these verses, Paul says that Christ "preached peace" to both Jews and Gentiles. Verse 17 is a quotation of Isaiah 57:19, in which Isaiah prophesied that the Lord would proclaim peace to those who were "far" and those who were "near." It might seem strange to say that *Christ* preached to both Jews and Gentiles, when the majority of his earthly ministry was to Jewish people in Israel. But this reality was fulfilled when Christ tasked his apostles, and the church in all ages, with taking his message of good news to the whole world. "Go therefore and make disciples of all nations,"

---

7   Quoted in Stott, *Message of Ephesians*, 92.

he commanded in his Great Commission (Matt. 28:19). If you're a Gentile who's heard the good news of true peace with God and man, it's because Christ himself preached it to you through one of his gospel emissaries.

As you read the Bible, it can sometimes be challenging to understand how God's Jewish people and his Gentile people relate to one another in redemptive history. But these verses make one thing clear: Both Jews and Gentiles have an important place in God's saving purposes, and he intends for them to be part of the same body, the church. This means we will value both Jews and Gentiles; take the good news of the gospel to all who are apart from Christ, whether Jew or Gentile; and establish churches where Jews and Gentiles worship our great God together.

In our day, humans make repeated efforts to foster unity among people groups. Attention to racial reconciliation and justice, efforts to resolve international conflicts, and intervention on behalf of mistreated groups are often worthy projects. We can certainly affirm what's good about those efforts while recognizing that human-engineered peace will always fall short of divinely wrought unity. "He himself is our peace," writes Paul, proclaiming that the basis of true and lasting unity is found only in God. What divided people groups need most is not human diplomacy or advocacy but the blood of Christ that brings people of all ethnicities near to him.

EPHESIANS 2:19–22

¹⁹ So then you are no longer strangers and aliens, but you are fellow citizens with the saints and members of the household of God, ²⁰ built on the foundation of the apostles and prophets, Christ Jesus himself being the cornerstone, ²¹ in whom the whole

structure, being joined together, grows into a holy temple in the Lord. ²² In him you also are being built together into a dwelling place for God by the Spirit.

Like a party host introducing two guests to each other, Paul in these verses puts one arm around believing Jews and another around believing Gentiles and says enthusiastically, *I'm excited you're both here! You're going to get along so well; you've got so much in common!* He then uses three images: They share the same country, the same family, and the same house. Through these pictures, he invites us all to appreciate the beauty of the church.

Paul says that the church of Christ is like a country and church members like citizens. Believers are "fellow citizens with the saints." Jewish believers, of course, had always been part of God's special nation, Israel, and so this image would be familiar to them. But Paul says Christ has established the church as a new kind of society. In the church, every member has equal standing as a citizen. There are no "strangers and aliens" among church members— no undocumented migrants, no tourists on temporary visas, no green-card holders—only full citizens of Christ's own kingdom. In this country, believers have the rights that belong to "the saints": complete security in their salvation in Christ and complete safety in his kingly rule over them.

Paul also says that the church is like a family; we are "members of the household of God." Again, Jewish believers would have understood this image and readily traced their family heritage back to Abraham, Isaac, and Jacob. Christ, though, declared a deeper family history: "Before Abraham was, I am" (John 8:58). If Jewish believers were tempted to rest on their genetic ties, Jesus proclaimed that Abraham's true children are those who sincerely follow him (Luke 3:8). Paul pictures the church as a new family, where all believers are equally valued children who share God as their Father. As members of this family, we have free access to the Father and assurance that he loves and cares for us.

Finally in these verses, Paul describes the church as a house: We are "being built together into a dwelling place for God." This house has a foundation; it rests on the word of God ("the apostles and prophets"). This means the church must look to the word of God to establish its contours. In any church, the members have the right to ask, Is this teaching consistent with the Bible? Is this practice? Is this priority? If it's not, the church must return to its foundation. The house Paul describes also has a "cornerstone" who is Christ. The cornerstone is a foundation stone that is placed at the corner of the building. It brings the walls together and gives the whole building stability. Paul says the church is a kind of living building that "grows" in Christ. Each person—Jew or Gentile, male or female, rich or poor—is like a stone that adds to the building. Without the cornerstone, we'd be unevenly spaced and wobbly, but Christ brings us together as a unified house. And this is a house with an inhabitant: "a holy temple" and "a dwelling place for God by the Spirit." Just as the temple was where God dwelt among his Old Testament people, the church is a new and living temple where God takes up residence. It would have been amazing to be present at the first temple's dedication when "the glory of the Lord filled the house of the Lord" (1 Kings 8:11). It's no less amazing to gather with the church on Sunday and to know that, together, the members are the "dwelling place for God."

You might be used to thinking of the Christian faith in largely individual terms. You might talk about your "personal" testimony or "personal" journey of faith. And it's true that following Christ *is* personal. The Lord tenderly calls each of his people to himself and works in her life in precise ways to make her more like himself. Each person trusts Christ personally; no one else can trust in Christ for her. But a passage like this one teaches us that Christ also sees us corporately—as his church. When he saves us, he unites us to all his people. It's his good design that we wouldn't live the Christian life alone but would be part of his country, his family, and his house. Paul's words in these verses are a welcome to us, too: *I'm glad you're here. You're going to love these people; you have so much in common!*

Ephesians 3

Gospel Mystery

¹ For this reason I, Paul, a prisoner of Christ Jesus on behalf of you Gentiles— ² assuming that you have heard of the stewardship of God's grace that was given to me for you, ³ how the mystery was made known to me by revelation, as I have written briefly. ⁴ When you read this, you can perceive my insight into the mystery of Christ, ⁵ which was not made known to the sons of men in other generations as it has now been revealed to his holy apostles and prophets by the Spirit. ⁶ This mystery is that the Gentiles are fellow heirs, members of the same body, and partakers of the promise in Christ Jesus through the gospel.

You probably know someone who gets distracted in conversation. She may start out telling you a story about what happened at the grocery store yesterday but then realizes she should explain why she was even *at* the grocery store at 7:30 a.m. buying carrots and chicken (to make a meal for her sick neighbor, as it turns out).

After she explains about the neighbor (who has always been pretty prickly, but maybe the chicken soup will help), she finally returns to her original point about the events at the checkout. Similarly, in Ephesians 3, Paul begins to tell the Ephesians that he's praying for them, but in verse 2, he has a Spirit-inspired distraction and gives the backstory to his calling as an apostle. He returns to his prayer later (v. 14), but in these verses, he explores the "mystery" of the Gentiles' inclusion in the church, which is the impetus for Paul's ministry among them.

In verse 1, before Paul changes tack, he reintroduces himself. He earlier identified himself as "an apostle of Christ Jesus by the will of God" (1:1), establishing his God-given authority. Now, he calls himself "a prisoner of Christ Jesus," revealing his deep submission to the Lord.[1] Paul was imprisoned in Rome at the time he wrote this letter. And yet he doesn't say he's "a prisoner of the awful Romans." Instead, he humbly acknowledges that he's both an apostle and inmate by the will of God. He is, ultimately, *Christ's* prisoner. This undoubtedly comforted him. He knew Christ was with him, he knew Christ had good purposes for him, and he knew Christ would release him (either in life or in death) at exactly the right moment (see Phil. 1:7, 12–14, 19).

What might it look like to emulate Paul's submission to God's providence? You're not simply a patient at the cancer center; you're *Christ's* patient. You're not answering ultimately to a difficult boss; you're working for *Christ*. You're not at the mercy of a negligent landlord; you live in *Christ's* kingdom. He's with you, he has good purposes for you, and he'll bring you out of your hard situation at just the right time.

---

1 Stuart Olyott, *Alive in Christ: Ephesians Simply Explained*, Welwyn Commentary Series (1994; repr., Evangelical Press, 2000), 78.

The second part of his introduction ("on behalf of you Gentiles") is where Paul breaks off to explain the backstory of his ministry. Paul had impeccable Jewish credentials (Phil. 3:5–6), and yet God made him "an apostle to the Gentiles" (Rom. 11:13). In fact, he was now in prison as a result of that ministry. He so highly values Gentile inclusion in the church that he is willing to suffer and even die as the price for being an apostle to them. In Ephesians 3:2–6, Paul explains that his unlikely calling is because of God's plan to proclaim the gospel to the Gentiles and include them in his church. Paul describes this using the language of "mystery." It's important to understand that while a "mystery" in the modern West typically means a secret that remains hidden, a "mystery" to Paul's first-century hearers was a secret that has been revealed or "made known." Paul explores this mystery in two parts: He explains how God revealed it (vv. 2–5), and he explains what it is (v. 6).

It makes the most sense for us to look first at Paul's definition of this mystery: "This mystery is that the Gentiles are fellow heirs, members of the same body, and partakers of the promise in Christ Jesus through the gospel" (v. 6). Paul uses three parallel Greek words—translated in English as the longer phrases we see here—to express the full inclusion of Gentile believers in the church. They are coheirs, comembers, and cosharers.[2] Gentiles, he says first, are "fellow heirs" with Jews. They equally receive the inheritance Paul described in 1:11–14: new life in God's kingdom now and the fullness of life forever with him in the future. Like the late-arriving workers in Jesus's parable of the vineyard (Matt. 20:1–16), the Gentiles may be newcomers, but

---

2 John R. W. Stott, *The Message of Ephesians: God's New Society*, The Bible Speaks Today (InterVarsity Press, 1979), 117.

they receive the same reward as the Jews. Next, Paul says Gentiles are "members of the same body." Together with the Jews, Gentiles are equally part of Christ's body, the church. And they belong to the *same* body; as Paul already affirmed, Christ made "in himself one new man in place of the two" (2:15). Finally, Paul says Gentiles are "partakers of the promise." Although the Jews had the early advantage of first receiving God's promises and covenants, the Gentiles can now share those same promises. When we read the Old Testament in light of the truths in these verses, we can see that God intended Jews and Gentiles to receive the fulfillment of his promises together. In the church, God dwells with Jews and Gentiles together and is their God (see Ex. 29:45).

All this is "in Christ Jesus through the gospel" (Eph. 3:6). Throughout Scripture, the mystery is always ultimately about the Messiah—the promised one who would be revealed in time to God's people.[3] In verse 6, Paul unfolds the final wrinkle in this tapestry, and we see it spread before us. The mystery is the Messiah, who, on the cross, secures the right relationship of Jews and Gentiles to God and to one another. The mystery is Christ who gathers his church.

Having seen what the mystery is, we can understand how Paul says it was revealed (vv. 2–5). If Ephesians was indeed a circular letter—passed around to several area churches—not everyone was necessarily familiar with Paul's story. And even if the letter wasn't intended for other churches, Paul hadn't been in Ephesus for ten years. There were certainly new members in the congregation who didn't know Paul personally. For their sake, Paul recaps what

3   Bryan Chapell, *Ephesians*, Reformed Expository Commentary, ed. Richard D. Phillips and Philip G. Ryken (P&R, 2009), 140.

some already knew ("assuming that you have heard"). "How the mystery was made known to me by revelation" probably alludes to his experience on the Damascus road, where Christ revealed himself to Paul and sent him to preach the gospel "before the Gentiles" (Acts 9:15; see also Acts 9:1–19; Gal. 1:12, 15–16). At that time, the mystery of Gentile inclusion in Christ became clear to Paul. In these verses, he highlights a few key things about the revelation of this mystery: First, the revelation wasn't his own idea; it was "given" to him by God (Eph. 3:2). Next, it wasn't given to him only for himself; it was a "stewardship" that he was given in order to give it to others. And it wasn't given only to Paul but also to the "holy apostles and prophets"—others who had been called by God to build up the early church. Finally, it wasn't an entirely new revelation, but it was revealed more fully to Paul than it had been in "other generations." Throughout the Old Testament, we see some incidences of Gentile inclusion (Ruth and Rahab, for example) and promises of expanded, future inclusion (for example, Isa. 56:7; 60:10–14). But, here, Paul announces a radical, complete unity of Jews and Gentiles in Christ and in his church.

Because of Christ, every member of your church has equal standing with every other member. The word is preached to every person in the room. God receives the prayers and praises of every believing heart. The Lord's Supper and baptism belong to all who are part of God's covenant people. Every person's gifts and graces are necessary; every person's needs are important. This Sunday, you too can behold the mystery: In the church, people of all ages, ethnicities, sexes, abilities, education levels, and socioeconomic backgrounds are joined together in Christ as coheirs, comembers, and cosharers!

7 Of this gospel I was made a minister according to the gift of God's grace, which was given me by the working of his power. **8** To me, though I am the very least of all the saints, this grace was given, to preach to the Gentiles the unsearchable riches of Christ, **9** and to bring to light for everyone what is the plan of the mystery hidden for ages in God, who created all things,

If you've ever walked down your street at night, you may have noticed how strange your house looks in the dark. Without lights or warmth, and from a distance, it's almost hard to recognize it. But once you get inside and flick on a lamp, it becomes the comforting place you know so well. So, too, once the "mystery" has been illuminated (vv. 1–6), we can see it clearly for what it is: the gospel.[4] In these verses, Paul explains how, having received the mystery of Christ who unites his church, it's been his life's work to proclaim it to the Gentiles as good news. Paul here tells the Ephesians about himself, about his message, and about his audience.

In describing himself, Paul emphasizes both his high calling and his low standing. He was "made a minister" by "the working of [God's] power." It's hard to imagine a more elevated calling. And yet he's "the very least of all the saints." It's hard to imagine a lower standing. The thread between the two is God's grace (vv. 7–8). Paul, the persecutor of God's people, was saved and included among the saints by grace alone (Acts 9:1–19; 1 Cor. 15:10). Paul, the fearless gospel preacher, was given his calling to ministry by grace alone ("according to the gift of God's grace"). God calls particular people

---

4 Stott, *Message of Ephesians*, 118.

and gives them particular tasks ("to *me* . . . this grace was given"), and it's always all because of grace.

Paul's message, too, is a study in contrasts. He preaches and brings to light the good news of Christ ("the plan of the mystery"). But his message is ultimately beyond words. It's the "unsearchable riches of Christ." Paul is called to preach, but no human (including Paul!) can fully comprehend the depths of the truths he's preaching. The good news of Christ, who unites his people to himself and to one another, is better and richer and greater than any of us can comprehend. In this life, and in the life to come, there will always be more to Christ than we have explored. And in every age, we will proclaim what we do not yet fully understand.

Finally, the audience for Paul's message is both narrow and wide. God called him to preach "to the Gentiles," and specifically to the Ephesians who received this letter. But Paul also knew that his ministry would have a greater reach than his own time and place; it would be for "everyone." This letter to the Ephesians wasn't a message to be read only by its original recipients—and then quickly forgotten. It wasn't even merely a circular letter for the first-century congregations. Paul knew his words would "bring to light for everyone what is the plan of the mystery hidden for ages in God." The Lord who "created all things" called Paul to preach the gospel, not only to the Ephesians but to people in far-off places and coming ages. How is that possible? Two thousand years later, we can personally testify to the fulfillment of this. *We* get to hear the gospel from Paul.

The main point of these verses is this: Paul counts it his life's highest privilege—and a grace of God—to tell others about Christ. And though we aren't given apostolic or even pastoral office in the church, we each have opportunities to proclaim "the unsearchable riches of Christ" to those around us. With our children, around our neighborhoods, at our workplaces, and in our Bible studies, we have a great privilege: to speak to others about Jesus. By God's grace, we get to shine gospel light on people who sit in darkness. Like Paul, we couldn't ask for a better calling!

EPHESIANS 3:10–13

10 so that through the church the manifold wisdom of God might now be made known to the rulers and authorities in the heavenly places. **11** This was according to the eternal purpose that he has realized in Christ Jesus our Lord, **12** in whom we have boldness and access with confidence through our faith in him. **13** So I ask you not to lose heart over what I am suffering for you, which is your glory.

So far in chapter 3, we've seen the mystery revealed (vv. 1–6) and then proclaimed (vv. 7–9). In verses 10–13, Paul explains the grand goal of all this. Once again, he pushes us to see the ultimate effect of the gospel, not merely in individual terms but in corporate ones. Christ reconciles sinners to himself in order to make them part of his church. And he makes people part of his church so the entire cosmos will see the glory of God. (A pretty amazing promise for a ragtag congregation on a rainy Sunday morning!)

By gathering his people into the church, Christ displays "the manifold wisdom of God." "Manifold" is a poetic word that means something like "many-sided" or "many-colored."[5] When people of all kinds (Jews and Gentiles, men and women, adults and children, wealthy and poor) come together in the church, we form an arrestingly varied congregation. The church includes people

---

5 Frank Thielman, *Ephesians*, Baker Exegetical Commentary on the New Testament (Baker Academic, 2010), 215.

with different stories of coming to Christ, possessing a variety of spiritual gifts, and given diverse "good works" (2:10) to walk in. Nowhere else in the world are people who are so different from one another brought together in such complete unity. This, in turn, reveals that our all-wise God is not dull or one-dimensional but is, like his church, beautiful and multifaceted. Each individual Christian is one snapshot of a life transformed by Christ—but it's only in the gathered church that the world can begin to glimpse the multicolored depths and riches of God's wisdom.

The audience for this display is none less than "the rulers and authorities in the heavenly places." It's the spiritual beings who worship continually before God's throne—the angels. Paul returns to the topic of spiritual beings in chapter 6, but here he explains how God "made known" to angels his saving purposes. Rather than *telling* the angels about it, he *shows* them in the church. In 1 Corinthians, Paul says we ought to be aware that angels are present in our worship gatherings (1 Cor. 11:10; see also Heb. 12:22), and this verse affirms that one reason they're there is to learn about God's wisdom. From eternity past ("according to the eternal purpose," Eph. 3:11), God intended that Christ's church would be a school for heavenly beings.

What's more, the church has unlimited access to God through the work of Christ ("boldness and access with confidence through our faith in him"). When we gather in the church, God speaks to us (in the reading and preaching of his word), and we speak to him (in song and prayer). Because of Christ, the "manifold wisdom of God" is intimately available to us.

These truths were meant to embolden the Ephesian church, and they should embolden us, too. In verse 13, Paul tells his hearers there's no need for them to be discouraged that he's in prison because of his ministry to the church. *What's a little suffering*, he encourages, *when the church displays the wisdom of God to the whole world and to the angels too?* We can remember this when serving the church is hard. It doesn't look glamorous at the time, but it's absolutely worth it when we set our eyes on God's glorious purposes for his people. No matter how ordinary your church seems, it has access to God and preaches to the cosmos.

EPHESIANS 3:14–16A

¹⁴ For this reason I bow my knees before the Father, **¹⁵** from whom every family in heaven and on earth is named, **¹⁶** that according to the riches of his glory

Remember the prayer Paul started in verse 1 and then abandoned? Finally, he's returning to it. He begins this section with the same language he used earlier ("for this reason . . .") and then continues with his prayer for the Ephesians. As with his prayer in chapter 1, Paul uses one long sentence in Greek for this entire prayer (vv. 14–19). In verses 14–16a, Paul introduces his prayer: why and how he prays, to whom he prays, and to what degree he expects God to answer.

The opening ("for this reason") points back to all that Paul explored in chapter 2—with the addition of his discourse in the first half of chapter 3. Paul has in mind the Ephesians' salvation from spiritual death by God's grace (2:1–10), the Gentiles' reconciliation to God and to his people by Christ (2:11–22), and the gospel message that was once hidden but now has been revealed and proclaimed in the church (3:1–13). These truths are so glorious that they've literally knocked Paul off his feet ("I bow my knees before the Father"). Although standing was the typical posture for prayer in Jewish worship, Paul is so overwhelmed that he falls to his knees.[6] And it's on the basis of these glorious realities that Paul prays for the Ephesians.

Paul prays to "the Father, from whom every family in heaven and on earth is named." Paul is awed by the glory and grace of God, but he nevertheless approaches him on intimate terms ("Father"). In our own prayers, too, we approach God as not only the great King but also the loving Father, as not only the Creator of all things but also as the Supplier of our needs, as not just the holy God but also as the Savior of sinners. God is a Father with a family, and Paul highlights that here. Though we might generally think of "family" as a mom and dad with kids, Paul means something broader here. He's talking about the spiritual family of believers with God as the Father. The translation "every family" may signify something like "each group" (God's spiritual family includes people from all ethnicities and nationalities, as well as those from all eras of history, and even all kinds of angelic beings in heaven). Alternatively, some would prefer to translate this phrase as "his whole family," which communicates the idea of "oneness" (God's spiritual family as it exists both in heaven and earth is a united whole).[7] Whichever is correct, each reflects a scriptural truth. God includes his people from every kind of group in his vast kingdom. And God brings his people together in one family—the church—under him as their Father. By creating them in his image and under his authority, God places his name on them, just as a human father gives his name to his children. The basis of Paul's prayer is that God cares about his church, so Paul asks him to bless it.

Finally, Paul sets up his prayer by affirming the degree to which he expects God to answer: "according to the riches of his glory."

---

6   Stott, *Message of Ephesians*, 132–33.

7   Stott, *Message of Ephesians*, 133; Peter T. O'Brien, *The Letter to the Ephesians*, The Pillar New Testament Commentary (Eerdmans, 1999), 255–56.

If a four-year-old in your Sunday school class asks what you'd like her to give you for your birthday, you aren't going to request much. A construction-paper card (sweet as it may be!) is probably the most extravagant gift she can produce. But if your millionaire uncle asks the same question, you won't hesitate to suggest diamond earrings. The Lord has immeasurable riches—all things are at his disposal—so Paul prepares to ask boldly. As the old hymn says,

Thou art coming to a King,
Large petitions with thee bring;
For his grace and power are such,
None can ever ask too much.[8]

[that] he may grant you to be strengthened with power through his Spirit in your inner being, [17] so that Christ may dwell in your hearts through faith—that you, being rooted and grounded in love, [18] may have strength to comprehend with all the saints what is the breadth and length and height and depth, [19] and to know the love of Christ that surpasses knowledge, that you may be filled with all the fullness of God.

What do you want most for yourself and for your loved ones? If prayer is "an offering up of our desires unto God,"[9] our prayer requests reveal our deepest longings. In the final verses of chapter 3,

8   John Newton, "Come My Soul, Thy Suit Prepare," 1779, in *Trinity Hymnal*, rev. ed. (Great Commission, 1990), 628.
9   Westminster Shorter Catechism, in *The Confession of Faith: Together with the Larger Catechism and the Shorter Catechism with Scripture Proofs*, 3rd ed. (Christian Education and Publications, 1990), q. and a. 98.

we get to see what Paul wants most for his Christian brothers and sisters in Ephesus. He asks God to grant them three things: strength, knowledge, and fullness.

Paul's first petition is for strength: "that . . . he may grant you to be strengthened with power." He doesn't have in mind physical strength here, since he asks for strength "in your inner being." In light of God's saving and reconciling grace—realities Paul explored in chapter 2 and in the first part of chapter 3—this is a prayer for spiritual might. It's strength to resist sin and persevere in righteousness. For this, they need "power." Such "power" has a Trinitarian source: It comes from the Father ("that . . . he may grant you") as the Son lives in believers by his Spirit ("through his Spirit . . . so that Christ may dwell in your hearts") through faith. As in Jesus's parable of the strong man, Christ must break into the house of our hearts, bind Satan, and take possession. Only then can we stand against evil (Matt. 12:25–30). God alone gives his people the ability to walk in the new life he's given them.

Paul's second petition is for knowledge: "that you . . . may have strength to comprehend . . . and to know the love of Christ." Paul begins this petition by picturing the Ephesians as a plant and as a building. He wants them to be "rooted" in love —to gain their stability and nourishment from it. He also wants them to be "grounded" in love—to rest on it as their foundation. (Commentators disagree about whether the "love" in verse 17 is Christ's love for believers or believers' love for Christ. Both themes are found in this letter, but, in the context, Christ's love seems more likely.)[10] Building on this foundation of love, the believers can then grow—to increase their knowledge of love. As in chapter 1,

---

10 Stott, *Message of Ephesians*, 136; O'Brien, *Ephesians*, 260.

Paul here wants the Ephesians to "know" in their minds as well as in their experience. What's more, Paul wants the Ephesians to know this love corporately ("with all the saints"). The believers are like homebuyers stepping into their new house and pacing out the dimensions of each room. As they measure the doorways and assess the height of the ceilings, they envision their life together in this amazing space. Paul prays for them to know "the breadth and length and height and depth" of Christ's love, but at the same time he acknowledges that it "surpasses knowledge." Believers must seek to know what they can never fully know. It takes "strength" to even begin to comprehend the vastness of our Savior's love for us. As John wrote, "the world itself could not contain" everything there is to know about Christ (John 21:25). Our new life in Christ is the life of an explorer: We are always pressing on to discover lengths and heights and depths we've never known before and yet, after we discover those, marveling that yet further vistas await.

Paul's third petition is for fullness: "that you may be filled with all the fullness of God." Paul used similar language in chapter 1, where he described the church as "the fullness of him who fills all in all" (v. 23), and he'll use it again in chapter 4, where he'll write about the church growing up into "the stature of the fullness of Christ" (v. 13). Here, Paul prays that the believers' increasing knowledge of Christ's love will lead to increasing spiritual maturity. Theologian D. A. Carson illustrates this truth with a personal anecdote about two siblings in foster care: The children moved frequently from house to house and floundered emotionally and intellectually until they settled with a loving family for a period of years. The stability and nurture of their final home gave them a safe place to begin to grow.[11]

---

11 D. A. Carson, *A Call to Spiritual Reformation: Priorities from Paul and His Prayers* (Baker, 1992), 195–97.

Likewise, once we're secure in Christ's love (from which "nothing can ever separate us," Rom. 8:38 NLT), we're in the best position to grow into spiritual maturity. We can study the Bible with renewed hearts, trusting that the unfolding story of Christ's redeeming work is true and good. We can pray, knowing that God hears us because of Christ. We can gather with the church for worship, believing that the church is where Christ gathers us in his presence. We can fight sin and pursue holiness, trusting that Christ is working in us. Year after year, we can flourish in our new life, knowing that Christ loves us.

EPHESIANS 3:20–21

²⁰ Now to him who is able to do far more abundantly than all that we ask or think, according to the power at work within us, ²¹ to him be glory in the church and in Christ Jesus throughout all generations, forever and ever. Amen.

Paul concludes his prayer for the Ephesians with a doxology—a short hymn of praise to God. Having asked God for big things, Paul praises him as the God who can do big things. This doxology also concludes the first half of Paul's letter to the Ephesians. The letter's first half was more theological; the second half will be more practical. This doxology, then, is the crescendo to his theology. Paul here confidently declares God's power, glory, and eternality.

Paul praises God as the one "who is able to do far more abundantly than all that we ask or think, according to the power at work within us." In that first phrase, nearly every word amplifies God's power. He is "able" to do what we ask—it's well within his power. What's more, he can do "all" that we ask. And not only can he do all we *ask*, but he can even do those things we've barely *thought* of ("all . . . we ask or think"). God knows us so completely that he knows both our carefully expressed requests and our half-formed thoughts and hopes. "He who searches hearts" understands our desires even when we don't know how to pray for them (Rom. 8:26–27). God is able to do all we ask or think, and he does it "abundantly" and "more" and even "far more" than we expect. Like so many who came to Jesus for physical healing and left with forgiveness of their sins, we always receive an answer to our prayers that goes deeper than our limited human imaginations anticipated. We ask for daily bread, and he feeds us with himself. We ask for a paycheck, and he lavishes on us unfading spiritual treasure. We ask for friends, and he comes alongside us and dwells with us. And he does these things "according to the power at work within us." He's a God of limitless power, and he works in us "according to" that power.

Paul also proclaims God's glory: "to him be glory in the church and in Christ Jesus." God is glorified everywhere in his creation; as the psalmist sang, "the heavens declare the glory of God" (Ps. 19:1). But in the church and the Son, God is especially glorified. In the church, he is revealed as Lord and King, as Shepherd and Savior, as the source of life itself. And in Christ Jesus, we see "the radiance of the glory of God and the exact imprint of his nature" (Heb. 1:3). In the church, God displays what he does. In Christ, he displays who he is. All of it brings him glory.

Finally, Paul declares that there's no end to God's power and glory. He will receive glory both "now" and "throughout all generations, forever and ever." From the moment we enter into new life in Christ, we will never stop praising God. And year after year, until Christ returns, God will keep adding worshipers to his church. Babies yet to be born will be singing this doxology long after this world has passed away. To these verses, our response must be "Amen." This is a word that means "yes" or "so be it." It's a believing assent, a faith-filled affirmation. With an "Amen," God's people throughout all generations sign their names to this doxology. *Yes. With my whole heart I know this is all true. I believe it, Lord, and I praise you for it.*

Ephesians 4

Life in the Church

¹I therefore, a prisoner for the Lord, urge you to walk in a manner worthy of the calling to which you have been called, ²with all humility and gentleness, with patience, bearing with one another in love, ³eager to maintain the unity of the Spirit in the bond of peace.

Chapter 4 opens the second—and more practical—half of Paul's letter to the Ephesians. In his final three chapters, Paul gives instructions for living out new life in Christ and in Christ's church. Paul expects that what his hearers have come to believe should affect the way they act. These verses at the beginning of chapter 4 lay out the way to pursue unity in the church. Here Paul gives two incentives, lists four virtues to cultivate, and encourages work toward one goal.

Paul's incentives to unity in these verses can be summarized like this: *I'm urging you* and *God is calling you*. Paul begins by emphasizing his personal commitment to Christ and his church ("I therefore, a prisoner for the Lord, urge you"). It isn't just anyone asking the Ephesians to cultivate unity; it's Paul. Paul is no ivory-tower academic who discusses hypotheticals with other elites while sipping tea. Paul is literally in chains because of his allegiance to Christ. The personal cost Paul's paying gives him the freedom to "urge"—beseech, implore, even beg—the Ephesians to work hard. It's always easier to accept a challenge from someone who's personally invested. A coach who has played the game and is willing to run drills with the team will get respect when she tells her athletes to give everything they've got. A boss who started at the company making coffee and copies will be better positioned to assign her employees grunt work now and then. Paul is forfeiting his freedom and his life for the sake of the gospel, so he's earned the right to ask the Ephesians to do hard things too.

Paul also says God is calling his people to unity ("walk in a manner worthy of the calling to which you have been called"). Earlier in this letter, Paul described the life to which God has called believers: salvation from spiritual death by God's grace (2:1–10), reconciliation to God and unity with his people through Christ (2:11–22), and knowledge of the gospel in the church (3:1–13). Now, he's telling them to act accordingly. Since believers have such a high calling, sinful actions and attitudes are beneath them. Instead, they ought to deliberately live up to the standards of life in Christ, "walk[ing] in a manner worthy" of their calling.

Paul then lists four virtues believers should cultivate: humility, gentleness, patience, and long-suffering. The first, "humility," or lowliness, characterizes a person who puts others before herself. Like Christ, who "humbled himself by becoming obedient to the point of death" (Phil. 2:8), we serve others at cost to ourselves. "Gentleness," or meekness, characterizes someone who treats others with kindness and avoids harshness and bitterness. Like Christ, who is "gentle and lowly in heart" (Matt. 11:29), we welcome others and are tender toward them. "Patience" and "bearing with one another in love" (Eph. 4:2) are related and characterize someone who endures the weaknesses and forgives the sins of others. Like the Lord, who is "slow to anger, and abounding in steadfast love and faithfulness" (Ex. 34:6), we show love to others, even when we've been wronged.

As the Ephesians increasingly practice these virtues (or what Christians often call "graces"), Paul urges them to be "eager to maintain the unity of the Spirit in the bond of peace" (Eph. 4:3). Believers don't create unity in the church; that's a reality secured by the Spirit. God already broke down "the dividing wall of hostility" and created "in himself one new man in place of the two, so making peace" (2:14, 15). But that doesn't diminish our responsibility to "maintain" what God has accomplished. By our Spirit-empowered efforts at humility, gentleness, patience, and long-suffering, we eagerly foster "the bond of peace" that sustains the unity God created. Mopping the floors and recaulking the shower don't build the house, but they prevent decay and make it a pleasant place to call home. In the church, our loving interactions with one another are the routine maintenance God's household needs to be a place where everyone can live well together.

EPHESIANS 4:4–6

⁴ There is one body and one Spirit—just as you were called to the one hope that belongs to your call— ⁵ one Lord, one faith, one baptism, ⁶ one God and Father of all, who is over all and through all and in all.

Look around your church on Sunday. Over there, you see a woman who's in a completely different life stage from you. Next to her is a family who has more money than you've ever seen in your life. In the back row is a group of college students who come from around the globe and speak languages you don't. Beside them is a man whose job is so specialized you've never understood what he does. In the whole congregation, there are just a handful of people (if that!) with whom you seem to have much in common. Your experience isn't a new one. In first-century Ephesus, the believers were a similarly diverse group. And yet, like every church in every age, they were called to unity. In these verses, Paul encourages unity by reminding believers that we have seven fundamental realities in common.

Many of these realities are truths Paul has already explained, but he piles them up here, as if to say, *Look how much you share!* Let's briefly consider each: (1) "There is one body," Paul begins, affirming that the church is a unified whole (see 1:22–23; 2:15–16). Each local congregation is a microcosm of the universal (worldwide, age-less) church to which all true believers belong and in which each member uses his or her gifts to contribute to the whole. (2) "One Spirit" refers to the Spirit of God, who gives unity to his church (see 4:3) and who dwells in the church. (3) Our "one hope" (v. 4; see also 1:12) is in the promise of Christ's coming and the future inheritance that awaits us. (4) We trust in and submit to "one Lord," Jesus Christ, who rules over all things and is head of his church. (5) And we profess "one faith," the truth expressed in Scripture and believed by all who are in Christ.[1] (6) The visible sign and seal of our belonging to God's people is "one baptism." It's true that churches differ in their practice of baptism, but, without dismissing our sincere and distinct convictions, we can affirm that baptism also

---

1 If your church service includes a corporate confession of faith—saying the Apostles' or Nicene Creed, for example—learn to savor that part of worship. Here is a group of people who might not agree about much but who together cling tightly to what matters most.

unites us. In baptism, water is the visible sign that sets us apart as God's holy people. (7) Finally, we glorify "one God and Father of all" (4:6; see also 1:2; 3:14–15), proclaiming together that there is no God beside him. This one God is "over all"; he reigns supreme in his creation and especially over his church (see 1:22–23). He is "through all"; through the church, he reveals his glory to the world and even to the heavenly beings (see 3:9–10). He is "in all"; by his Spirit, he dwells in his church (see 2:22).

These seven truths compel us to unity. That woman or those teenagers in your church may not seem to have much in common with you, but you actually share the most important things in the world. Education, ethnicity, wealth, sex, age, employment, and personality each lose their power to divide us when we remember that Christ died for us, gives us new life in him, unites us to himself and one another, and promises us an unfading inheritance. You have more in common with the people in your church than with anyone else in the world.

EPHESIANS 4:7–8

7 But grace was given to each one of us according to the measure of Christ's gift. **8** Therefore it says,

> "When he ascended on high he led a host of captives,
>   and he gave gifts to men."

Unity doesn't mean uniformity, however.[2] Christians aren't cookie-cutter versions of each other, and Scripture nowhere says we should

---

2 Stuart Olyott, *Alive in Christ: Ephesians Simply Explained*, Welwyn Commentary Series (1994; repr., Evangelical Press, 2000), 99.

be. Instead, having declared the doctrines that believers hold in common, Paul now turns to the gifts that make us unique. He begins in verses 7–8, then breaks off in verses 9–10 for a related theological reflection, then returns to the theme of gifts in verses 11–12. In verses 7–8, Paul affirms the existence of spiritual gifts and identifies their recipients, explains the gifts' extent, and traces their source.

The word "grace" (*charis*) and "gift" (*charismata*) are closely related in the Greek text, and Paul uses "grace" here to mean spiritual gifts that serve the church.[3] "Grace was given to each one of us," Paul says, and, later, "he gave gifts to men." God gives exactly the right gifts in exactly the right measure to exactly the right people at exactly the right time for the good of the local church. In this way, even though our gifts are diverse, they still foster unity. "Each one of us" has gifts from the Lord to be used for the good of his church (see 1 Cor. 12:4–7). And when we come to the gifts of public leadership in the church mentioned in verses 11–12, we'll see that Christ gifts exactly the right people for that work too.[4]

Next, Paul explains the gifts' extent: "according to the measure of Christ's gift." This is good news for us. We aren't drawing our gifts from a dwindling supply. Christ has the Spirit "without measure" (John 3:34; see also Rom. 12:3), and so he has all the Spirit's gifts (spiritual gifts) in their fullness. It's according to his immeasurable gift and his manifold wisdom (Eph. 3:10) that he gives us our gifts. If we have a particular gift—wisdom, perhaps,

---

3   John R. W. Stott, *The Message of Ephesians: God's New Society*, The Bible Speaks Today (InterVarsity Press, 1979), 155.

4   A few sentences in this paragraph are adapted from my book *A Place to Belong: Learning to Love the Local Church* (Crossway, 2020), 80–81.

or generosity—we may not think we have it abundantly. We sometimes struggle to know how to counsel others, or we see so many other places we could have given resources. But our gifts from Christ are like top-of-the-line tools. If we don't immediately use them at full capacity or wield them as skillfully as we'd like, it's not because the gifts are lacking. Instead, as we practice and mature, we'll grow into them.

Finally, Paul traces our spiritual gifts' source to the ascended Christ. Quoting Psalm 68, Paul paints the picture of a conquering king distributing the spoils of war to his loyal subjects. The king ascended to his throne, leading captives and surrounded by lavish gifts. Christ our king also ascended to God's right hand after his death and resurrection, and he leads us, his "host of captives" with him. Thankfully, we aren't imprisoned captives in chains but redeemed captives who are about to be given gifts. (We'll have to wait until verses 11–12 to see the gifts Paul particularly highlights: gifts of proclaiming God's word.) You may notice that Paul says Christ "gave gifts to men" (4:8), but Psalm 68 says "receiving gifts among men" (Ps. 68:18). It's possible that Paul deliberately changed the language to emphasize Christ's generosity toward us, and it's also possible that both giving and receiving are understood in Ephesians 4 and Psalm 68. The victorious king receives gifts as tribute and then gives them to those under his command.[5]

Presidential collections are full of gifts from other heads of state, but I doubt that many ordinary citizens have ever received a gift from a king or queen. Even fewer have received a gift from a monarch who knows and loves them, has stayed in their home,

---

5   Stott, *Message of Ephesians*, 157.

and has personally chosen that particular gift for them especially. And no one has ever received a royal gift that will never diminish or run out. Except for us. These verses teach us that our ordinary churches, full of ordinary people, are the recipients of gifts beyond measure from a king who will reign forever.

EPHESIANS 4:9–10

⁹(In saying, "He ascended," what does it mean but that he had also descended into the lower regions, the earth? ¹⁰ He who descended is the one who also ascended far above all the heavens, that he might fill all things.)

As he's done before, Paul here breaks his train of thought to meditate on a particular theological point. Verses 9–10 are Paul's commentary on his quote from Psalm 68. He clarifies the meaning of "ascended" as a contrast to Christ's descent, and then he explains the implications of Christ's ascension.

Paul begins by contrasting ascension and descension—making the logical case that what goes up must have, at some point, been down. Paul argues that Christ's ascension to the right hand of God necessarily means "that he had also descended into the lower regions, the earth." Commentators throughout Christian history have proposed various interpretations of this descent. Some older theologians connected it with 1 Peter 3:19 ("in which he went and proclaimed to the spirits in prison"), which they associated with Christ going to Hades, or hell. But there's no reference to hell in these verses (or in 1 Pet. 3), and more recent commentators reject that interpretation. Instead, Paul is probably talking about Christ's incarnation (his taking on human flesh and becoming a man) or, more broadly, what theologians call Christ's "state of humiliation" (all the indignities and limitations of life as a man in a fallen world). It's also possible that "descended" specifically refers to his death on the cross—the lowest point of Christ's earthly life.[6] Whatever the correct interpretation, Paul makes the point that Christ's ascension is a glorious reversal of his earlier condition. He was seen merely as a man and is now revealed as God. He was lowly and is now exalted. He was dead and now lives forever.

And Christ's ascension has implications for the cosmos. Paul uses superlative language to describe Christ's exalted place: "far above all the heavens." No part of the physical universe or the spiritual realm is outside his dominion. In similar language to his words in 1:23, Paul says Christ ascended so that "he might fill all things." Although it may not be obvious to the world, he is ruling over everything. From this exalted position, then, he's able to give abundant and fitting gifts to his people.

EPHESIANS 4:11

¹¹ And he gave the apostles, the prophets, the evangelists, the shepherds and teachers,

Like siblings racing to the tree on Christmas morning, we're now going to see what's in the gifts we've been told are for us (vv. 7–8). The letter to the Ephesians is a letter for (and largely about) the church, so we're right to assume these gifts will be for the whole congregation to enjoy. We've also been told that they come from

---

6   Stott, *Message of Ephesians*, 158–59.

Christ ("he gave")—who once was in our place on earth and now is exalted to a position of power over all things (vv. 9–10). We're therefore also right to assume that these gifts will be exactly what people in our situation need and will be better than we can imagine. In this part of chapter 4, Paul tells us what the gifts are (v. 11), and then he explains what they're intended to do and why we need them (vv. 12–14).

Let's unwrap our five gifts: "the apostles, the prophets, the evangelists, the shepherds and teachers." They're each an office (or public ministry role) in the church. The "apostles" were a small group of specially appointed men who lived at the time of Christ's earthly ministry and in the early days of the church. They included Jesus's twelve disciples (minus Judas), Matthias, James, Paul himself, and perhaps a few others (Acts 1:12–26; Gal. 1:19; Eph. 1:1). These men were commissioned by Christ (Eph. 1:1), were eyewitnesses of his resurrection (Acts 1:22; 1 Cor. 9:1), were infallible and authoritative as they taught and wrote the New Testament Scriptures (1 Thess. 2:13), and were confirmed in their apostolic calling by the miracles they performed (2 Cor. 12:12).

"The prophets" refers to people who were mouthpieces or spokespersons for God. They weren't *foretellers* so much as *forthtellers*. What God gave them to say, they told forth for the good of God's people. The Old Testament names many prophets, but Paul here is likely talking about New Testament prophets who used their gifts in the early church (Acts 13:1; 1 Cor. 14). We no longer have prophets or apostles today. Now that the New Testament Scriptures have been completed, we have all the words from God we need. As we saw in chapter 2, the church was "built on the foundation of the apostles and prophets" (v. 20); since the foundation has been built, we don't need to keep expanding it. But, although these offices existed only in that brief period after Christ's ascension while the church was being established, we still benefit today from their ministry through the scriptures they wrote.

The final three gifts are offices that continue in the church today. "Evangelists" are people particularly gifted to proclaim and explain the gospel to unbelievers. The church sends out evangelists to preach the gospel where it hasn't yet been preached or to organize churches where they haven't yet been planted. In the New Testament, both Philip and Timothy are described as evangelists (Acts 21:8; 2 Tim. 4:5). The next two gifts, "the shepherds and teachers," share one article ("the"), so some commentators think the words describe the same office. There is overlap between the roles, but they are not synonymous. Shepherds—elders who care for the "flock" (1 Pet. 5:1–3)—do their pastoral work in part by teaching the word of God to the church (1 Tim. 3:2; 2 Tim. 2:24). Teachers—those gifted in explaining God's word—may serve in the church or be sent by the church to do their work in other contexts like seminaries or schools. So, all shepherds must be teachers, but not all teachers are shepherds.[7] In your church today, your pastor and elders are some of the "shepherds and teachers" that Paul describes, and you regularly benefit from their ministry of God's word as they preach and teach.

In the New Testament, we find five different lists of spiritual gifts (Rom. 12:6–8; 1 Cor. 12:8–10, 28–30; Eph. 4:7–11; 1 Pet. 4:10–11). Each writer has chosen to feature particular gifts while leaving off others. None of these lists is meant to be exhaustive. Paul's list in Ephesians highlights gifts with God's word at their center. Apostles, prophets, evangelists, shepherds, and teachers are

---

7 Stott, *Message of Ephesians*, 163–64.

all ministers of God's word. As we'll see in the next verses, that's exactly what the church needs.

¹² to equip the saints for the work of ministry, for building up the body of Christ, ¹³ until we all attain to the unity of the faith and of the knowledge of the Son of God, to mature manhood, to the measure of the stature of the fullness of Christ, ¹⁴ so that we may no longer be children, tossed to and fro by the waves and carried about by every wind of doctrine, by human cunning, by craftiness in deceitful schemes.

Have you ever received a gift that left you scratching your head? Maybe it was a gadget or tool whose usefulness wasn't immediately obvious to you. We trust that the five gifts in chapter 4 are perfect for us—they're given to us by the ascended Christ, after all! But to help us understand why Christ gave the church these particularly, Paul explains what these gifts are intended to do and why we need them.

Christ gives gospel ministers to the church to build up the body into maturity. By writing, preaching, and teaching God's word, they "equip the saints for the work of ministry." Some commentators believe verse 12 contains three synonymous tasks for the church's word ministers that should rightly be separated by commas. If so, the verse would read, "to equip the saints, for the work of ministry, [and] for building up the body of Christ." Other commentators believe the verse describes a single task in which ministers equip church members to use their own gifts in the church for the good of the church. Either interpretation expresses a truth from this text, and it's difficult to know which is prefer-able. The existence of the list of public ministry roles in verse 11 affirms that those men have a special, authoritative, Christ-given, word-based ministry—a ministry that's distinct from what others do in the church. Like literal shepherds, they care for the flock by feeding, guiding, and protecting the sheep. But Paul's teaching in verses 12–16 emphasizes a church body where "each part is work-ing properly" (v. 16), inferring that the members each contribute to the ministry as they serve in the church. In both ways, Christ builds his church.

Ultimately, the work of gospel ministers fosters the church's maturity. Here, Paul picks up on themes he's already discussed: "the unity of the faith" (see also 4:1–6) and "the knowledge of the Son of God" (see also 1:16–19; 3:18–19). As God's servants min-ister God's word to God's church in the power of God's Spirit, we increase in these things and become mature. Like young siblings aspiring to match their older sibling's pencil-marked height mea-surements on the wall, we continue growing until we reach "the measure of the stature of the fullness of Christ." When you look at your church, it may seem hard to believe this will ever happen. But the good news of these verses is that the church's maturity is assured. Christ is going to continue using the apostles' teaching and raising up elders in his church until we "attain" maturity. What's more, none of Christ's redeemed people will be left behind. We "all" will attain it. Increasingly in this life and completely in the next, Christ's church will mature.

Finally, Paul explains why we need these gifts: On our own, we'd never grow up. Children need parents. If they're going to learn to use proper table manners, do a load of laundry, politely greet the neighbors, and ride a bike, they need mature adults to help them. In the same way, believers need spiritual parents ("so that we may no longer be children"). God gave us his word through the apostles and prophets, and he also gives us evangelists, shepherds, and teachers to help us understand and apply his word. This protects the church against instability. As we know, children are both fickle and gullible. One minute they think some fashion or hobby or product is great; the next minute they've completely rejected it. Often, that's because another kid has swayed them. It's a mark of maturity to become more stable and less susceptible to peer pressure. In the same way, believers can lack firm convictions ("tossed to and fro by the waves and carried about by every wind of doctrine, by human cunning, by craftiness in deceitful schemes"). One minute a certain doctrine or spiritual practice catches our fancy; the next minute, it's something else. This doesn't create a steadfast faith, and, worse, it leaves us vulnerable to the schemes of Satan and his wicked servants, false teachers. Instead, we need the testimony of the apostles from the past and mature gospel ministers today to help us develop convictions rooted in Scripture.

The pastors and elders in your church may seem like fairly ordinary men. They sincerely love and serve Christ, but they also struggle with sin and weakness like the rest of us. That's why it's essential to remember that these men are the gifts of Christ and that their ministry is proclaiming God's word. Because Christ gave them, we receive them. Their ordination to office is simply recognizing and affirming what Christ has already given. And they don't direct the church according to their own opinions. Whatever they preach or teach that's true from Scripture ought to be received as God's word to us (see 1 Thess. 2:13). This is how the church grows up.

EPHESIANS 4:15–16

¹⁵ Rather, speaking the truth in love, we are to grow up in every way into him who is the head, into Christ, **¹⁶** from whom the whole body, joined and held together by every joint with which it is equipped, when each part is working properly, makes the body grow so that it builds itself up in love.

In our day, some people pride themselves on being "truth" people. They say it like it is, call out falsehoods wherever they hear them, and sometimes consider it necessary to trample on others' feelings in service to honesty. Other people value being "love" people. They prioritize relationships and feelings, and so they try not to cause offense. Sometimes they even willingly downplay truth claims in order to demonstrate care for others. Christians, however, are truth *and* love people. In these verses, Paul describes the mature church as a place where members hold firmly to the truth, act in love, and work together for the good of the whole body.

By emphasizing the importance of those who proclaim God's word, Paul has already affirmed our need for truth. Gospel ministers' preaching and teaching shape our convictions and keep us from being the storm-tossed children from verse 14. Now, Paul says that members of the congregation, too, have an obligation to speak "the truth" to one another. While preaching may be the special calling of the church's elders, having spiritual conversations and studying the Bible with others is a job for every believer. It's perfectly appropriate for us to talk about the weather or our hobbies with people in the church, but how much more should we talk together about what the Lord says in his word? Our church building's hallways and classrooms, and its members' kitchens and front porches, ought to ring with the sounds of Scripture being quoted, discussed, and applied. And we should do it "in love." Love is a committed affection for another that seeks that person's good above her own. Whatever biblical truth we say, we say it with affection and motivated by the other person's good. We don't compromise the truth, but we also don't skimp on love. Individuals, and even whole congregations, can be more naturally "truth" people or "love" people, but part of maturing is growing into both. Immaturity produces lopsidedness; maturity produces a congregation that "speak[s] the truth in love."

Next, Paul again says we mature to match Christ ("grow up in every way into him who is the head, into Christ," see also v. 13). You've probably noticed how a baby's head is disproportionately large for her body. It's not until she grows up that her body and head become equivalent. Paul uses the image of a body with Christ as its head. As it matures, the body starts to grow up in proportion to its perfectly mature head. The head, Christ, equips all the parts ("from whom the whole body, joined and held together by every joint with which it is equipped"). He gives the church everything it needs to flourish. And the members use the gifts and resources they've been given to care for one another ("when each part is working properly, makes the body grow so that it builds itself up in love"). The picture is of a perfectly proportionate, healthy body—every part doing what it was designed to do. Under Christ, truth and love work together, God's people work together, and the body thrives.

There are two other lessons we can note from these verses: First, spiritual maturity isn't an individual pursuit. A lung or heart can't survive on its own and is generally useless apart from the body. We grow to maturity in the church, and never apart from it. Sitting under the preached truth and learning to love the people in the pews is the school for Christian maturity. Second, the church is the primary place we live out our new life in Christ. Belonging to Christ certainly has implications for how we conduct ourselves in our homes and neighborhoods and workplaces (and Paul will get to all those shortly!), but our life in the church is foundational—it sets the direction and pattern for all other situations.[8] If truth and love characterize our life in the church, they ought to characterize our life everywhere.

EPHESIANS 4:17–19

[17] Now this I say and testify in the Lord, that you must no longer walk as the Gentiles do, in the futility of their minds. [18] They are darkened in their understanding, alienated from the life of God because of the ignorance that is in them, due to their hardness of heart. [19] They have become callous and have given themselves up to sensuality, greedy to practice every kind of impurity.

When you go for a hike in unfamiliar territory, it's crucial to have a map. Otherwise, your walk down a seemingly pleasant path may eventually lead straight to a treacherous cliff or raging river. In the second half of chapter 4, Paul hands the Ephesians a trail map as they set out on the Christian life. He warns them of dangers (4:17–19) and then directs them to a better way (4:20–5:2). Paul is no casual day-tripper but an authoritative guide ("this I say and testify in the Lord"). The apostle cautions against four steps the Gentiles take in their path to destruction: a darkened mind, a hard heart, separation from God, and a debauched life. (It's worth noting that commentators disagree about the logical order of the four. The clauses

---

8 Olyott, *Alive in Christ*, 104.

are grammatically connected, but it's not clear exactly how. In any case, these steps are each part of the Gentiles' descent to judgment.)

Previously in this letter when Paul talked about "the Gentiles," he used the term to mean people who are not ethnic Jews, and he emphasized the unity of both Gentiles and Jews in the church (see 2:11–22). Here in 4:17–19, he's using "Gentiles" to mean pagans in general, and he's emphasizing the sinful condition of people without God. He's not telling Gentile converts they need to stop being Gentiles; he's telling all believers they need to stop acting like unbelievers ("you must no longer walk as the Gentiles do").

The first step Gentiles take toward destruction is with their intellect. Gentiles' minds are characterized by "futility," they are "darkened in their understanding," and "ignorance . . . is in them." This is willful ignorance (see Rom. 1:18). Unbelievers, no matter how many letters they have after their names, don't think straight about the most important truths in the world. They may study quantum physics, but they refuse to seek the universe's Creator. They may master a dozen languages, but they don't use them to praise God. They may design incredible houses, but they deliberately ignore the "builder of all things" (Heb. 3:4).

The next step happens in the Gentiles' hearts. Toward spiritual things, they have "become callous" and demonstrate "hardness of heart." Like Pharaoh in the days of Moses who was stubbornly impervious to both Yahweh's invitation and warning (see Ex. 8:32), unbelievers refuse to submit to the Lord. Even if they seem like upright, speed-limit-abiding citizens, their hearts are in spiritual rebellion. Neither God's invitations to mercy nor his threats of judgment have any effect on them.

As a result of their sluggish minds and stubborn hearts, Gentiles are "alienated from the life of God"—they have none of the benefits that God gives his children. While believers who know and love the Lord are "filled with all the fullness of God" (3:19), unbelievers in their ignorance and rebellion are "dead" (2:1), separated from the only source of true life.

Finally, they give "themselves up to sensuality, greedy to practice every kind of impurity." The invisible reality of the Gentiles' spiritual condition eventually becomes visible. Up to this point, it's possible that observers couldn't tell how bad it had gotten in the Gentiles' souls. But now, having internally rejected right thought, a tender heart, and God himself, the unbelievers' outward actions begin to spiral. They pursue "sensuality" (prioritizing their own pleasure) and "every kind of impurity" (flagrantly transgressing God's law). They've given up. In his parallel passage in Romans 1, Paul says of unbelievers that "*God* gave them up" (v. 28). Both statements are true. Unconverted people don't care about pleasing God and eventually give up attempting right conduct. Also, God's patience toward them runs out, and he gives up restraining them. It's hard to imagine anything worse.

EPHESIANS 4:20–24

20 But that is not the way you learned Christ!— **21** assuming that you have heard about him and were taught in him, as the truth is in Jesus, **22** to put off your old self, which belongs to your former manner of life and is corrupt through deceitful desires, **23** and to be renewed in the spirit of your minds, **24** and to put on the new self, created after the likeness of God in true righteousness and holiness.

As he's done before in this letter (2:4, 13), Paul snatches his hearers back from despair with the blessed word "but." In those earlier statements, Paul affirmed that God changes our condition (we were once dead but are now alive) and our relationships (we were once alienated but are now united). Here, Paul declares that God changes our behavior (we were once corrupt but are now holy). In verses 20–21, he explains the basis for new conduct: Christ's work. In verses 22–24, he lays out the pattern for new conduct: putting off wickedness and putting on godliness. Then, in the rest of chapter 4, he'll list specific examples of what newness of life looks like.

Paul may be emphasizing our right conduct, but he grounds it in Christ's work. We depend on Christ in order to move from death to life. We depend on him to move from alienation to union with God and his people. And we depend on him so we can stop acting like unbelievers and start acting like our God. We have "learned Christ"—Christians are those who know Christ. Christ is the very center of the gospel. We have also "heard about him and were taught in him." Following from verses 11–14, Christians hear about Christ through the eyewitness testimony of the apostles, recorded in Scripture and proclaimed by the preaching and teaching of gospel ministers in the local church. We are also "taught *in* him"—receiving his word by his Spirit. Ultimately, "the truth is in Jesus." When we come to know Christ, that knowledge affects how we understand everything. Christians act in a particular way because they've been changed by a particular person.

Paul describes the radical change in believers' conduct like a change of clothes. If you were a prisoner and then became a surgical nurse, you'd need a new uniform. You'd take off your orange jumpsuit and put on a pair of blue scrubs. Your changed life would be obvious to everyone. So, too, believers "put off" the "old self." This is that dim-witted, hard-hearted, God-alienated, evil-loving self that Paul describes in verses 17–19. It was displayed by a sinful "former manner of life" and was rotten ("corrupt") right down to its core ("deceitful desires"). Having "put off" the uniform of our past life, we "put on the new self." In Christ, we exchange our former ignorance (v. 18) for being "renewed in the spirit of [our] minds." We "learned Christ," and so now we can understand life rightly. Even Christians whom the world judges neither smart nor educated know the deepest truth of the universe: Christ saves sinners. What's more, we're now "created after the likeness of God." We were once "alienated from the life of God" (v. 18), and now we're being remade to reflect his character. And whereas our old self gave herself up to "every kind of impurity" (v. 19), our new self pursues "true righteousness and holiness." Dear Christian, don't lose heart. You may have once walked in Gentile ways, but now Christ is making you completely new.

EPHESIANS 4:25

²⁵ Therefore, having put away falsehood, let each one of you speak the truth with his neighbor, for we are members one of another.

For the rest of chapter 4, Paul lists several ways our new self ought to act. Remember, these commands are not divorced from Christ. Paul's "therefore" points back to his theological teaching in verses 20–24. We do these things in obedience to Christ, out of gratitude for Christ, and according to the power of Christ at work in us. In our practice as in our belief, Christ is everything.

Verse 25 commands us to use godly speech. We "put away" lies and deception, and we "speak the truth." This is a way we honor others and affirm our relationship with them. The person to whom we are speaking is our "neighbor" (and the Lord repeatedly commands us to love our neighbors; for example, Matt. 22:39). What's more, the person is part of the church with us: "We are members one of another." Like Ananias and Sapphira (Acts 5:1–11), we might be tempted at times to make ourselves look better than we are to the rest of the congregation, but this isn't good for anyone. The unity that Christ accomplished in his church (Eph. 2:11–22) is lived out when his people create a culture of trust and love by speaking only what is right. In Christ, liars become truth tellers.

26 Be angry and do not sin; do not let the sun go down on your anger, **27** and give no opportunity to the devil.

Everyone in the church is learning to put off the old self, so it's not surprising that we occasionally get angry at one another. Paul doesn't forbid all anger; Jesus himself was sometimes angry (see Mark 10:14; John 2:13–17). We're right to be angry about the things God hates. But, Paul says, don't let your anger express itself in sinful ways, and don't let your anger go on too long. Being angry is no excuse for unkindness or rage. And being angry is no reason to let a grudge fester or bitterness take root. Those are practices of our past life; we used to give ourselves up to sin (Eph. 4:19). If we fall back into those patterns, Satan will try to destroy us ("give no opportunity to the devil," Eph. 4:27; see also 1 Pet. 5:8). Instead, we must bring even our anger into submission to the Lord and resolve our conflicts in righteous ways (see Matt. 5:22–24; 18:15–17). In Christ, hot-tempered people become self-controlled people.

28 Let the thief no longer steal, but rather let him labor, doing honest work with his own hands, so that he may have something to share with anyone in need.

Each person in Christ's church isn't who she used to be. Everyone has an "old self" (v. 22). Here, Paul says that if your old self was someone who took things that didn't belong to you, your new self should stop stealing and instead seek to give things to people who need them. The problem with stealing is twofold: It's taking what belongs to someone else, and it's refusing to work. Christians, though, ought to respect one another's property (Ex. 20:15) and work "heartily, as for the Lord" (Col. 3:23). Work isn't usually glamorous and is often difficult, but if it's "honest" (not something contrary to God's law) and you do it yourself ("with his own hands"), it honors the Lord. Work also allows you to be generous ("so that he may have something to share with anyone in need"). The church ought to be a place where believers with resources give to believers without them, even "begging . . . earnestly" to be allowed to contribute (2 Cor. 8:4; see also Acts 2:44–45). In Christ, takers become givers.

29 Let no corrupting talk come out of your mouths, but only such as is good for building up, as fits the occasion, that it may give grace to those who hear.

Paul has plenty to say about how Christians should talk. He's already told us that we should speak "the truth in love" (v. 15) and "speak the truth" rather than falsehood (v. 25). Here he tells us we should put off "corrupting talk." The word for "corrupt" means "rotten," like rotten wood or rotten fruit.[9] This includes unkind speech that tears others down and vulgar speech that introduces decay into others' minds and hearts. Because conversation is a relational act, we should have others in view. We must put on godly speech with three characteristics: "good for building up," "fits the occasion," and "give[s] grace to those who hear." In contrast to the rottenness of rude words and filthy words, righteous words encourage others to godliness. In contrast to the thoughtless stream of evil words, righteous words are carefully chosen. And in contrast to the profanity of wicked words, righteous words imitate our Lord's grace. Maybe you used to be someone who insulted others or who regularly cursed. Now you can be someone whose words produce good. In Christ, the foulmouthed become edifying.

EPHESIANS 4:30

30 And do not grieve the Holy Spirit of God, by whom you were sealed for the day of redemption.

Here Paul momentarily pauses his specific directions to make a broader theological point. In verse 27 he warned the believers against giving "opportunity to the devil," and in verse 30 he warns them not to "grieve the Holy Spirit." In a list that focuses on visible actions, these cautions remind us that our outward behavior has spiritual implications. Resuming the sinful patterns of our old way of life will invite Satan to attack our souls. And acting in unrigh-

---

9   Stott, *Message of Ephesians*, 188.

teous ways will grieve God himself. In this verse, Paul highlights two reasons God hates believers' sin: First, *God* is holy. He's "the Holy Spirit of God," and so our unholy conduct is directly opposed to his nature. Second, *we* are holy. We've been "sealed for the day of redemption"—redeemed by God and set apart to God—and so our unholy conduct is directly opposed to our new identity. There's both a present and future reality in Paul's words. We "were sealed for the day of redemption"—we're holy now, and on the day of Christ's return we'll be confirmed in perfect holiness forever. On that day, we'll no longer sin, and the danger of grieving our gracious God will be no more. Come, Lord Jesus!

EPHESIANS 4:31–32

31 Let all bitterness and wrath and anger and clamor and slander be put away from you, along with all malice. 32 Be kind to one another, tenderhearted, forgiving one another, as God in Christ forgave you.

Paul now resumes his list of practical imperatives by returning to the theme of church conflict. In verses 26–27, he focused on our need for self-control. In these verses, he highlights our need to extend forgiveness. We "put away" all kinds of bad attitudes toward others: "bitterness" (a sour spirit), "wrath" (uncontrolled rage), "anger" (ongoing resentment), "clamor" (shouting and screaming), "slander" (spreading a bad report), and "malice" (wishing harm to others).[10] It's not hard to see how any one of those is harmful in the church! Instead, we ought to "be kind" (seeking others' good),

---

10 Stott, *Message of Ephesians*, 190.

"tenderhearted" (compassionate), and "forgiving" (releasing others from the penalty for their wrong against us). Paul isn't forbidding any pursuit of justice (passages like Matt. 18:15–17 lay out that process), but he is saying that our new self ought to be inclined to forgiveness wherever possible. We were once spoiling for a fight; now we're rooting for reconciliation. Paul began his list of commands with an appeal to Christ ("therefore," v. 25), and he also ends it with one. We forgive others because God forgave us ("as God in Christ forgave you"). Like the servant in Jesus's parable, we've been forgiven an unpayable debt and therefore ought to forgive the much smaller debts of others (Matt. 18:21–35). In Christ, grouches become gracious.

Ephesians 5

Walk in Love

¹Therefore be imitators of God, as beloved children. ²And walk in love, as Christ loved us and gave himself up for us, a fragrant offering and sacrifice to God.

The first two verses of chapter 5 are logically connected to the second half of chapter 4. Chapter 4, verse 24 ("put on the new self, created after the likeness of God"), and chapter 5, verses 1 and 2 ("be imitators of God"), are like bookends. In between, Paul lists specific commands. The bookends clarify the purpose of the intervening commands. Whether we're resolving our conflicts quickly (4:26) or choosing our words carefully (4:29), we're ultimately aiming for godliness. Godliness means being godlike—loving what God loves, hating what he hates, and acting in holy ways. And though we'll never *be* God, we seek to be *like* God by imitation. God is our Father, and we are his "beloved children." Just as children look up to their parents and try to be like them, we honor God and imitate him (see Matt. 5:48). Christ, as God incarnate, is also our example. He "loved us and gave himself up for us," and so too we love and serve those around us. Christ's self-sacrifice and ours are "a fragrant offering and sacrifice to God." This encourages us when people don't seem to notice or care that we've given ourselves for their good. God sees. Our efforts to "walk in love" rise before him like sweet-smelling smoke from an offering.

EPHESIANS 5:3–4

³ But sexual immorality and all impurity or covetousness must not even be named among you, as is proper among saints. ⁴ Let there be no filthiness nor foolish talk nor crude joking, which are out of place, but instead let there be thanksgiving.

Having exhorted the believers to "walk in love" (v. 2), Paul now warns against sins that stem particularly from its opposite: selfishness. Believers must put off "sexual immorality" (sexual intercourse outside marriage), "impurity" (all sinful sexual behavior), and "covetousness" (sinfully desiring what belongs to someone else; in this context it may especially mean desiring someone else's body or spouse).[1] Each of these sins aims to please the self rather than serve others. These sins "must not even be named among you," Paul says (see also v. 12). Obviously, Paul's just named them himself, so he's not forbidding saying those terms. Instead, he's warning believers not to make them a subject of casual conversation or to dwell on them. It's not "proper" for "saints" (see also 1:1, 4) to fill their mouths and minds with unholy things. If we do, we may become

---

1 Andrew T. Lincoln, *Ephesians*, Biblical Word Commentary, ed. Bruce M. Metzger (Word Books, 1990), 321–22.

so comfortable with those sins that we're even tempted to make light of them. "Filthiness" (obscenity), "foolish talk" (degrading speech), and "crude joking" (sexually charged jokes)[2] objectify other people and cheapen God's good gift of sex for the sake of a laugh. This is "out of place" among believers who've been made new. "Instead," Paul says, "let there be thanksgiving." Rather than wanting what we can't have, we thank God for giving what's best. Rather than pleasing ourselves at others' expense, we praise the one who "gave himself up for us" (v. 2). Rather than desensitizing others to sin, we invite them to worship our holy God. In Christ, pleasure grabbers become thanksgivers.

EPHESIANS 5:5–6

5 For you may be sure of this, that everyone who is sexually immoral or impure, or who is covetous (that is, an idolater), has no inheritance in the kingdom of Christ and God. **6** Let no one deceive you with empty words, for because of these things the wrath of God comes upon the sons of disobedience.

Throughout the Old Testament, wild parties are often the occasion for God's sudden judgment. In the days of Noah, godless humanity feasted and celebrated until the very moment when the flood swept them away (Matt. 24:37–39; see also Gen. 6:11–13; 7:21–23). In ancient Babylon, King Belshazzar and a thousand pagan friends drunkenly partied in the palace until God's finger appeared and wrote judgment on the wall, and Belshazzar was killed (Dan. 5). Even God's own people frolicked at Mount Sinai around their

2 Peter T. O'Brien, *The Letter to the Ephesians*, The Pillar New Testament Commentary (Eerdmans, 1999), 360–61.

golden calf until they encountered the Lord's immediate, consuming wrath (Ex. 32; see also 1 Cor. 10:6–8). It's all fun and games until God appears in judgment. These verses in Ephesians are similar to those Old Testament narratives. In Ephesians 5:3–4, everyone was having a laugh together, joking about illicit sex; in verses 5–6, the revelers stand condemned to eternal judgment. Paul's warning here is perhaps the most sobering of any in this letter. He says that willful sinners have no part in God's kingdom and are under God's wrath.

"For you may be sure of this," Paul begins. Like Jesus's "truly" (e.g., Matt. 10:15; 18:3), Paul's phrase emphasizes the veracity of what he's about to say. Then, echoing his mention of "sexual immorality and all impurity or covetousness" from Ephesians 5:3, Paul says, "everyone who is sexually immoral or impure, or who is covetous (that is, an idolater)," is under judgment. Although you may not love studying grammar, you should notice it here. In verse 3, Paul describes sins. In verse 5, he describes sinners. This tells us he's now talking about people who willfully and habitually practice these evils. These sins are so much a part of sinners' lives that it's accurate to call the people themselves "immoral" and "impure." They want the object of their sinful desire so fervently that they essentially worship it, making them "idolater[s]." Paul isn't talking about the believer who stumbles into sin, is convicted by the Spirit, genuinely repents, and then pursues new obedience (albeit imperfectly). He's talking about people who have "given themselves up" to wickedness (4:19) and who make sin their normal way of life. In contrast to the "beloved children" of God (v. 1), habitual sinners are "sons of disobedience."

For such people, Paul has a sobering word: They have "no inheritance in the kingdom of Christ and God." They won't share in the inheritance the Spirit guarantees to those who are in Christ (see 1:11–14). Instead, because of their grievous patterns of unrepentant sin, "the wrath of God comes upon" them. Tolerating sin invites disaster. In our day, many deny the reality of eternal punishment for those who reject the God of the Bible. It was the same in the first century. Paul cautions, "Let no one deceive you with empty words"—don't listen to those who downplay the existence of hell and judgment. It's not a comfortable thought that people who choose a life of sin will suffer the just consequences forever. But Paul's purpose here is ultimately redemptive. To the child happily running after her ball as it bounces across the street, it seems excessive, even harsh, to be jerked back from the curb by her screaming mother. But her mother has seen the truck barreling down the road. *Watch out!* Paul shouts. *Judgment is just around the corner!*

We might wonder why Paul particularly highlights the sins of sexual immorality and covetousness as those that bring God's wrath. Elsewhere in Scripture, it's clear that every sin deserves God's just judgment. As Paul himself writes, "The wrath of God is revealed from heaven against *all* ungodliness and unrighteousness of men" (Rom. 1:18). Sexual sin and greed deserve God's wrath. So do dishonoring authority and taking the Lord's name in vain. It's true, though, that some sins are particularly grievous—either because of their extreme nature or because other sins come with them.[3] Paul elsewhere calls sexual sins especially heinous: "Every other sin a person commits is outside the body, but the sexually immoral person sins against his own body" (1 Cor. 6:18). Paul may be making that same case here by singling out such sins. But it seems more likely that Paul has chosen to focus on sexual

---

3   Westminster Shorter Catechism, q. and a. 83, says, "Some sins in themselves, and by reason of several aggravations, are more heinous in the sight of God than others." Westminster Shorter Catechism, in *The Westminster Confession of Faith Together with the Larger Catechism and the Shorter Catechism with Scripture Proofs*, 3rd ed. (Christian Education and Publications, 1990), 25.

immorality and covetousness because they are so directly opposed to his earlier command to "walk in love, as Christ loved us and gave himself up for us" (v. 2). Using people for our own pleasure and wishing their possessions were ours instead stands out as the evil opposite of Christ's self-giving love.

These verses raise one more issue we should consider. Why does Paul warn *believers*—the same group of people whose inheritance he has already called secure ("In him we have obtained an inheritance," 1:11)—of the dangers of hell? Does that mean a Christian's inheritance isn't guaranteed after all? First, remember Paul is writing to the church, and every congregation includes both believers and unbelievers (see Matt. 13:24–30). Some of the people sitting in Ephesus on Sunday morning listening to Paul's letter were "sons of disobedience." They may have walked into church, but they hadn't yet run to Christ. Also, Paul knew that even professing believers can presume on God's mercy—taking grace for granted and letting sin slide. Jesus says that, on the last day, some who thought they were righteous will have to acknowledge that they weren't truly following Christ (Matt. 7:21–23). Ultimately, Paul's grim warning is an opportunity to reflect. As he wrote to the Corinthians, "Examine yourselves, to see whether you are in the faith" (2 Cor. 13:5). Are you sincerely seeking, by the help of the Holy Spirit, to kill sin and imitate Christ? If so, be encouraged that your inheritance is secure. If not, today is the day of salvation, and Christ is the very great Savior. Leave your sin and flee to him!

EPHESIANS 5:7–14

⁷ Therefore do not become partners with them; ⁸ for at one time you were darkness, but now you are light in the Lord. Walk as

children of light [9] (for the fruit of light is found in all that is good and right and true), [10] and try to discern what is pleasing to the Lord. [11] Take no part in the unfruitful works of darkness, but instead expose them. [12] For it is shameful even to speak of the things that they do in secret. [13] But when anything is exposed by the light, it becomes visible, [14] for anything that becomes visible is light. Therefore it says,

> "Awake, O sleeper,
>   and arise from the dead,
>   and Christ will shine on you."

You probably know the old Bible study adage: When you encounter a "therefore," ask yourself what it's "there for." Paul has just finished warning his readers against the grave dangers of habitual sin—especially sexual immorality and covetousness—and it's with awareness of sin's seriousness that he now instructs the Ephesians how they should relate to people who've made those evils their way of life. These sins lead straight to eternal punishment; *therefore*, believers shouldn't dabble in them or casually hang around with people who practice them. To illustrate this, Paul uses a metaphor: the contrast between light and dark.

In these verses, Paul appeals to believers on the basis of their new life in Christ. "At one time you were darkness," he writes, "but now you are light in the Lord." Not only are believers "children of light" who "walk" in the light, but they *are* light. Paul affirms that when we are "in the Lord," Christ so radically changes us that our very identity is transformed. We will then display evidence of our changed nature; "the fruit of light" grows in our lives, and we "walk" in our new identity. We love what is "good," do what is "right," and believe what is "true." We also seek to know and do "what is pleasing to the Lord." Our light-filled life shines brightly and clearly through our conduct.

The opposite of light is, of course, "darkness." As Paul explained in chapter 4, unbelievers are "darkened in their understanding," alienated from the Lord, and callous toward the things of God (vv. 17–19). Life apart from Christ doesn't produce what is good, right, and true, but is, instead, "unfruitful." It bears nothing of value.

In this fallen world, light will eventually encounter darkness. As you go to school or work or even just as far as your own mailbox, you'll meet people who've rejected God and made sin (perhaps especially sexual sins and covetousness, v. 5) their normal way of life. How should you interact with them? Paul gives both negative and positive commands. He begins by saying, "Do not become partners with them." Paul doesn't forbid relationships with unbelievers: Inevitably, we have unbelieving coworkers, unbelieving neighbors, and unbelieving family members. We ought to maintain peace with them as far as it depends on us (Rom. 12:18) and seek their good (Gal. 6:10). But what Paul *does* forbid is participating with them in sin: "Take no part in the unfruitful works of darkness." We shouldn't commit sexual sins with them; nor should we "partner" with them by going along when they make crude jokes, describe sexual perversions, or express sinful desires. Paul also says it's "shameful even to speak of the things that they do in secret" (see also v. 3). Unbelievers' wicked exploits are not a fitting subject for believers' casual conversation or entertainment. Ultimately, Paul's warnings teach us that our relationships with unbelievers can be profitable (more on that in a minute), but they will never be easy. We deceive ourselves if we think light can simply hang out and have fun with darkness. As Proverbs warns, "Can a man carry fire next to his chest and his clothes not be burned?" (6:27). Because sin brings judgment, and because we are susceptible to temptation, we must be on high alert as we interact with unbelievers.

Paul also gives a positive command: We shouldn't participate in unbelievers' sins, but instead we should "expose them." Paul explains, "When anything is exposed by the light, it becomes visible, for anything that becomes visible is light." His logic is somewhat hard to understand, but he seems to be saying that believers should expose sin so that the exposed sinner can be changed. When sin remains unexamined and unacknowledged, the sinner doesn't recognize its seriousness and won't flee to Christ for cleansing. But when believers illuminate the true state of unbelievers, unbelievers may be saved. One of the tools in our evangelistic approach should be pointing out the danger of a life of sin.

This is the grim state of all who are apart from Christ: They are darkness. That might seem like a harsh thing to say about our unbelieving friends and neighbors, but Paul begins and ends this section on a hopeful note. In verse 8, he reminds the Ephesians that *they* were once darkness but now are light. And in verse 14, he celebrates the transformation the gospel offers to all people: "Awake, O sleeper, and arise from the dead, and Christ will shine on you." (Commentators disagree about the source of Paul's quote, but it may be a verse from a first-century hymn based on Isaiah 26:19 and Isaiah 60:1–2.)[4] Christ can—and does!—change people. Yes, we may need to relate to unbelievers with caution, but we can

---

4 Lincoln, *Ephesians*, 318–19.

also relate to them with hope, calling those in darkness to trust in Christ and be made light.

¹⁵ Look carefully then how you walk, not as unwise but as wise, ¹⁶ making the best use of the time, because the days are evil. ¹⁷ Therefore do not be foolish, but understand what the will of the Lord is.

If you've ever had surgery or recovered from an injury, you may have gone to physical therapy. Your therapist helped you to use your limbs correctly and effectively, sometimes after a long period of immobility. In the same way, our new life in Christ means we must learn to walk—to master the skill of moving through the world. So far in chapter 5, Paul has taught the Ephesians to "walk in love" (v. 2) and to "walk as children of light" (v. 8). In love, they are to give themselves in the church for one another's good. In light, they are to beware sin and call unbelievers to trust in Christ. Now, he instructs them to walk in wisdom. In wisdom, they are to spend their days intentionally, diligently, and obediently.

"Look carefully . . . how you walk," commands Paul. *Pay attention! Don't let the day's activities pull you along blindly. Don't let ungodly people drag you into their plans. Don't let your own sinful indifference allow you to act without thought. Look carefully!* Repeatedly in this chapter, Paul has urged attentiveness: "Be imitators"—notice what God is like and seek to be like him (v. 1); "try to discern"—study God's word and learn what pleases him (v. 10). Here, he similarly urges believers to deliberate action: "Look carefully," be "wise," and "understand." No one ever just happened to follow the Lord without realizing it. New life in Christ demands intentionality.

As those who pay attention, we should be "making the best use of the time." Our days have been numbered by our Lord (Ps. 139:16), and we must use each of them for his glory. We do this because "the days are evil" (Eph. 5:16). Each passing hour has the potential to be wasted—or, worse, spent in sin. Aware of this, believers do everything they can to redeem every moment to serve Christ. This doesn't mean believers never rest. The fourth commandment, for example, establishes a pattern of six days of work and one day of rest (Ex. 20:8–11). The "best use" of the time is sometimes hard work unto the Lord (see Col. 3:23) and sometimes intentional rest in the Lord. Every day presents opportunities, and we must seize them. New life in Christ demands diligence.

To do all this requires wisdom, and these verses tell us we become wise when we "understand what the will of the Lord is." If we want to avoid being "unwise" and "foolish," we need to know our God and what he requires. As Proverbs explains, "The fear of the LORD is the beginning of knowledge; fools despise wisdom and instruction" (1:7). Theologians talk about God's *secret will* and his *revealed will*. His secret will is his particular, sovereign design for each moment. (This includes things like whether God will heal your chronic illness, how he'll answer your prayers for a job, and whether he'll give you children.) We won't know his secret will until after it's come to pass. His revealed will, on the other hand, is what he says is pleasing to him (see 5:10). This is something we *can* know because he tells us in his word. (It includes things like the Lord's instructions from chapter 4 to speak truth, resolve anger, stop stealing, and be kind.) If we want to walk in wisdom, we'll study God's will revealed in his word—and ask the Spirit to help us understand and do what God says. New life in Christ demands obedience.

EPHESIANS 5:18–21

[18] And do not get drunk with wine, for that is debauchery, but be filled with the Spirit, [19] addressing one another in psalms and hymns and spiritual songs, singing and making melody to the Lord with your heart, [20] giving thanks always and for everything to God the Father in the name of our Lord Jesus Christ, [21] submitting to one another out of reverence for Christ.

In the early 1700s, Reverend Danforth of Taunton, Massachusetts, described a period of revival in his community: "We are much encouraged by a universal and amazing impression made by the Spirit of God on all sorts among us, especially the young men and women. . . . The young men," he wrote, "instead of their merry meetings, are now forming themselves into regular meetings for prayer, repetition of sermons, and singing."[5] Such stories are common in the history of revival. Where the Spirit goes, bars empty and churches fill, obscene jokes fade and hymns swell, drunken parties disband and worshipers assemble.[6] Because of the Spirit's work, even young

5   Heman Humphrey, *Revival Sketches and Manual in Two Parts* (New York, 1859), 63.
6   For example, in Ireland in the mid-1800s, one pastor reported, "There is an Orange Lodge in this neighborhood which is composed of some forty young men. They meet monthly and each contributed a fixed sum at every meeting for the purposes of procuring refreshments, which consisted almost entirely of whiskey. So much as £13 has been expended in one year in this way. They now meet principally for religious exercises—singing, prayer, or reading God's Word. They continue their monthly contributions and twice since July have asked me to expend a very considerable sum for the purchase of books for a library which they have established, and which is likely very soon to contain a large and very valuable collection of books. Now they never have any intoxicating drinks in their meetings." In

men—not the likeliest of choirs!—begin to gather for the purpose of praising the Lord. In these verses, Paul forbids coming under the influence of alcohol, which produces debauchery, and instead commands believers to come under the influence of the Spirit, which produces fellowship, worship, thanksgiving, and humility.

Paul begins with a clear prohibition: "Do not get drunk with wine, for that is debauchery." Paul elsewhere permits moderate alcohol consumption (see 1 Tim. 5:23), but what he's forbidding here is drunkenness. Alcohol masters the drunk person; it influences her thinking, her actions, and her speech. It leads to "debauchery," sinful behavior characterized by lack of self-control. Whether she's drinking to create a good time or to endure a difficult one, a drunk allows alcohol to control her. Those who are "slaves of God" (Rom. 6:22) ought not to be "slaves to much wine" (Titus 2:3).

Instead ("but"), believers should "be filled with the Spirit." Being "filled with the Spirit" is distinct from the baptism and sealing of the Spirit, which occur at the moment of conversion. The Lord gives his Spirit to believers on the day they first believe; as part of their new life in Christ, they should desire the Spirit's filling. This filling is his ongoing work in them, leading to their sanctification (or, increasing holiness). Notice here that all believers must seek to be filled with the Spirit; it isn't a special gift reserved for some. Notice also that this is

---

Scotland, around the same period, another pastor wrote, "I leave it with you to judge how far such facts make it evident that the work is from God; that vain persons who minded no religion, but frequented taverns and frolics, passing their time in filthiness, foolish talking and jesting or singing paltry songs, do now frequent Christian societies for prayer, seek Christian conversation, talk of what concerns the soul, and express their mirth in Psalms hymns and spiritual songs." A third pastor, again in Ireland, reported, "In passing through districts where the noisy laughter of the fool, or the impure language of the profane was wont to be heard, the voice of Psalms caught the ear in all directions." J. B. Johnston, *The Prayer-Meeting, and Its History, As Identified with the Life and Power of Godliness, and the Revival of Religion* (Pittsburgh, 1870), 305, 162, 306.

a continual command (its results include "giving thanks *always and for everything*");[7] it isn't reserved for a special circumstance. Finally, we'll see in a minute that it leads to self-controlled, holy action; in contrast to drunkenness, it isn't wild abandon. In Christ, substance-influenced people become Spirit-influenced people.

Paul now describes three effects the Spirit has on those he fills. First, believers speak to "one another in psalms and hymns and spiritual songs." This is a picture of Christian fellowship. The filthiness, foolish talk, and crude joking (v. 4) of our unbelieving past give way to songs that help others worship the Lord. The terms Paul uses ("psalms and hymns and spiritual songs") are not easy to differentiate, but together they indicate corporate singing in the worship gathering.[8] Although we may tend to think of singing as a personal act of worship, Paul reminds us that our Lord's Day praise instructs others about God and encourages them to praise him too. What's more, Paul commands worship "with your heart." Before we became Christians, we may have merely gone through the motions of worship. Now, filled with the Spirit, we sing out of sincere love for God and to encourage God's people.

The Spirit's next effect is thanksgiving. We give "thanks always and for everything to God the Father in the name of our Lord Jesus Christ." The idea here is that, for believers, thanksgiving is a continual, habitual way of life. "God the Father" has secured our salvation and our relationship to him "in the name of our Lord Jesus Christ," and so we have every reason to always give thanks!

The final effect of being filled with the Spirit is humility. We "[submit] to one another out of reverence for Christ." The Greek

---

7 The Greek verb for "be filled" is in the present imperative—it's an ongoing action. Stott, *Message of Ephesians*, 209.

8 Stott, *Message of Ephesians*, 205.

word for "submit" has, at its root, the Greek word for "order." As commentator John Stott explains, "Submission is a humble recognition of the divine ordering of society."[9] In different contexts, the Lord gives some people positions of authority and other people positions under them. In the church, he appoints elders to rule and requires the congregation to receive their leadership (Heb. 13:17). In civil society, he appoints government officials to rule and requires the citizens to obey (Rom. 13:1–3). In the home and the workplace (as we'll see in the next sections of Ephesians), he also establishes an order. As believers, we've already submitted our whole lives to Christ, and so, "out of reverence for Christ," we humbly submit to others when God places them in authority over us. And whether we are in authority or under authority, we "do nothing from selfish ambition . . . but in humility count others more significant than [ourselves]" (Phil. 2:3). The unbeliever often makes herself the center of everything and insists on her rights, her opinions, her plans. By contrast, the Spirit-filled person humbly seeks to serve others in submission to Christ.

EPHESIANS 5:22–24

²² Wives, submit to your own husbands, as to the Lord. ²³ For the husband is the head of the wife even as Christ is the head of the church, his body, and is himself its Savior. ²⁴ Now as the church submits to Christ, so also wives should submit in everything to their husbands.

By this point in Paul's letter, it should be obvious that our new life in Christ is so completely different from our old self that it

9   Stott, *Message of Ephesians*, 218.

changes everything. We were dead—and now are alive (2:1–10). We were alienated—and now reconciled to God and one another (2:11–22). We were ignorant children—and now equipped in the knowledge of Christ (4:1–16). We were liars, thieves, perverts, bullies, fools, and drunks—and now walking in love, light, and wisdom (4:17–5:21). "Submitting to one another" (5:21), then, is another feature of the Spirit-filled life that breaks from our old way of living. Once we did what pleased ourselves; now, "out of reverence for Christ" (v. 21), we do what serves others in the roles God gives us. This is such a significant shift in our way of living that Paul slows down and devotes greater space to explaining where and how we should submit. Submission informs how we relate to one another in the church (as we saw in vv. 18–21), and it also shapes the home and the workplace. In each of the next sections, Paul will specifically apply this command to a pair of roles: wives and husbands (5:22–33), children and parents (6:1–4), and bond-servants and masters (6:5–9). (It's worth noting that these sections mirror Paul's instructions in Colossians 3:18–4:1.) In Ephesians 5:22–24, he instructs married women to submit to their husbands.

Paul's command is simply put: "Wives, submit to your own husbands, as to the Lord." Later Paul will give instructions for other relationships. At any one time, a particular woman will likely assume several roles; she may be simultaneously a wife, a parent, and an employee. At an earlier point in her life, she was unmarried and a child. In the future, that woman may take on responsibilities as an employer; also, her husband may die, and she will no longer be a wife. Her identity in Christ is primary and constant (see Gal. 3:28; Col. 3:11), but she lives out her ultimate submission to Christ in specific ways in the different roles the Lord places her in at different times. The command in Ephesians 5:22 is specifically for "wives."

It's not for all women, but for women who are currently married. Paul also says, "Submit to *your own husbands*." He's not requiring all married women to submit to all married men. He's instructing wives how to act as believers in their own marriages to their own husbands.

What wives are to do in this command is "submit." As we noted in verses 18–21, the Greek word for "submit" has, at its root, the Greek word for "order." The wife who submits to her husband lives according to God's order for the family. Elsewhere, Paul (not to mention the rest of Scripture!) gives other directions for marriage. Wives and husbands should love one another (Eph. 5:25–33; Titus 2:4). They should pray together (1 Cor. 7:5). They should be faithful to one another (1 Cor. 7:10–13; Eph. 5:31). They should give and receive sexual pleasure together (1 Cor. 7:3–5). They should raise their children in the Lord together (Eph. 6:1–4). A God-honoring marriage includes many duties. Here, Paul focuses on submission because he's teaching the Ephesians how to live under God's order as those who submit to Christ. In the original Greek, there's not even a verb in verse 22 because the verb is already in verse 21. He literally says: "submitting to one another out of reverence for Christ. Wives, to your own husbands, as to the Lord."[10] If believers are to submit to one another in the roles God gives them, then one expression of this is the duty of wives to submit to their husbands. They do this "as to the Lord," under Christ's command and for his glory.

Paul goes on to explain the order God established in marriage: "For the husband is the head of the wife even as Christ is the head of the church." In God's divine decree, Christ is the head of the church (1:22–23; 4:15), and a husband is the head of his

10 Frank Thielman, *Ephesians*, Baker Exegetical Commentary on the New Testament (Baker Academic, 2010), 372.

wife. Because husbands and wives are both created by God in his image, they have equal dignity and worth. The intrinsic value of both is affirmed in this passage: Both husbands and wives were part of the congregation in Ephesus and present in the gathering; both husbands and wives received instructions from Paul, which they each are asked to freely obey; both husbands and wives are compared to something of immeasurable worth (husbands to Christ and wives to the church); and both husbands and wives serve one another as an expression of their greater service to the Lord. Husbands and wives have equal standing before God. They also have distinct roles. Paul gives three dimensions to Christ's role, which inform the dimensions of a husband's role. He is the "head," which indicates authority. He takes the church as his "body," which indicates union. And he is the "Savior," which indicates self-giving love. In response to these things, the church "submits to Christ"—humbly recognizes his authority and obediently serves him. "So also," Paul writes, "wives should submit . . . to their husbands." As an expression of her humble submission to God, a wife accepts her husband's authority, commitment, and care, and she seeks to serve him.

Finally, wives should submit to their husbands "in everything." Paul's command is expansive. A wife ought to be inclined to do what her husband asks, to live according to his priorities for their home, to receive his provision for her, and to joyfully serve him however she is able. Just as believers "try to discern what is pleasing to the Lord" (v. 10), wives seek opportunities to please their husbands. Paul's command is expansive, but it's not unlimited. A wife's submission to her husband is an expression of her ultimate submission to the Lord. This means she submits to her husband's authority as far as his directions are according to "the will of the

Lord" (v. 17). A husband doesn't have God-given authority to forbid righteousness or to require sin. In everything—including marriage—believers must serve Christ.

If a wife submitting to her husband seems radical, it is. Our new life in Christ upends everything about how we conduct ourselves, including how we relate to one another in marriage. If you're a wife, the command to submit to your husband is an opportunity to trust the Lord that his design is both right and good. Did he rescue you from spiritual death and slavery to sin and make you alive? Did he bring you out of isolation and give you a place to belong in his church? Did he protect you from Satan's lies by giving you apostles and shepherds to teach you truth? Did he release you from the influence of sin and fill you with his Spirit? Has he only ever done what is best for you? Well, then, can you trust him in this, too?

EPHESIANS 5:25–30

25 Husbands, love your wives, as Christ loved the church and gave himself up for her, 26 that he might sanctify her, having cleansed her by the washing of water with the word, 27 so that he might present the church to himself in splendor, without spot or wrinkle or any such thing, that she might be holy and without blemish. 28 In the same way husbands should love their wives as their own bodies. He who loves his wife loves himself. 29 For no one ever hated his own flesh, but nourishes and cherishes it, just as Christ does the church, 30 because we are members of his body.

Paul now turns to husbands: "Love your wives." As with his instructions to wives, Paul speaks here not to all men generally in their relationships to all women but to married men in their relationship to the wives God gave them. As we also noted earlier, Scripture as a whole prescribes several duties to husbands and wives that contribute to a God-honoring marriage. The wifely submission and husbandly love in this chapter are two of them. Remember, Paul's focus here is how new life in Christ transforms everything in a believer's life. A wife apart from Christ may be tempted to live autonomously and to stubbornly resist her husband's leadership. And so, in Christ, Paul instructs her to submit. A husband apart from Christ may be tempted to live autonomously and to selfishly exploit his wife's submission. And so, in Christ, Paul instructs him to love. Taken together, the two commands draw the couple into a self-giving relationship ordered according to the Lord's design—a relationship that pictures Christ and the church. In these verses, Paul uses two examples to teach husbands how to love their wives, one spiritual and one temporal: Christ's extraordinary love for the church, and a person's ordinary love for his own body.

Paul says husbands should love their wives "as Christ loved the church." Verses 25–27 explore several dimensions of Christ's love: (1) Christ "gave himself up"; from eternity past, he set his love on his people and determined to leave his heavenly throne to come as a man and die for the church's sake. As Paul writes in Philippians, "though [Christ] was in the form of God, [he] did not count equality with God a thing to be grasped, but emptied himself, by taking the form of a servant, being born in the likeness of men. And being found in human form, he humbled himself by becoming obedient to the point of death, even death on a cross" (2:6–8). Christ gave up his heavenly status to become man, gave up his life as a man in order to die, and gave up his dignity and rights in death as he died on the cross. (2) He gave himself up "for her, that he might sanctify her." Christ sacrificed himself in order to make the church holy ("that she might be holy"). He does this "having cleansed her by the washing of water with the word." "Water" refers to baptism—the sign and seal of our belonging to Christ and his church. "Word" refers to Scripture—God's revelation that sanctifies us by pointing us to Christ and directing us in the paths of obedience (see John 17:17). In the church, Christ communicates his love to the church, through the ordinances of the church. (3) Finally, Christ's goal is nothing less than the church's perfection: "so that he might present the church to himself in splendor, without spot or wrinkle or any such thing, that she might be holy and without blemish." Christ's love makes the church lovely. All her needs are supplied in Christ; all her desires are fulfilled in Christ. As he withholds nothing good from her—even giving her his own Spirit—her sins diminish, and her gifts blossom. Under his selfless love, she becomes beautiful. And, on the day of his return, he will "present the church to himself in splendor." The book of Revelation tells us the church in eternity will be holy and radiant, aglow with the presence of God, honored by the world's peoples, and freed from all sin (see 21:9–27). Christ's humility secures the church's glory.

If Paul's first example for husbands is astoundingly grand, his second is strikingly ordinary: "Husbands should love their wives as their own bodies." If a husband eats and drinks and gets dressed and makes sure to get enough sleep and avoids dangerous situations—"nourishes and cherishes" his own body—then he should do the same for his wife. This is an application of Jesus's teaching, "You shall love your neighbor as yourself" (Matt. 22:39). But it's even more than that. A husband loves his wife as his own body, and he loves her because she *is* his own body ("He who loves his wife loves himself," Eph. 5:28). When a husband and wife are joined in marriage, they become one. Paul will reinforce this in verse 31, but for now, he fuses it with his earlier example. A husband loves his wife because she is his body, just as Christ loves the church "because we are members of his body."

From these two lessons, husbands can see their duty. A husband ought to love his wife radically—withholding nothing that would be good for her, encouraging her spiritual well-being, and fostering a relationship with her where she flourishes. A husband also ought to love his wife in all the mundane ways—diligently looking out for the everyday good of her body, mind, and soul as he does for himself.

These verses tell us as much about Christ and the church as they do about husbands and wives. As members of the church—part of Christ's own body!—we should give thanks for the self-giving love of our Savior and resolve to submit to him in everything. We should rejoice in the union we have with Christ, a union closer even than that of a husband and wife. And in a culture where we're tempted to think of spiritual realities only in personal terms, it's particularly important to appreciate the corporate emphasis of these verses. The grand goal of Christ's redemption is not ultimately to save individual sinners but to gather and perfect the church. Jesus didn't come merely to save you; he came to make you part of his church. Although your local congregation may struggle at times, this passage testifies that Christ is at work there. On the last day, the church will not be the bruised and bedraggled group you see on Sunday mornings. She will be radiant and lovely, perfect and complete. Let the church's promised future encourage you today. Christ loves the church, works on behalf of the church, and promises to one day fully reveal the glory of the church. Your seat in church is nothing less than a front-row seat to Christ's redeeming work. You don't want to miss witnessing it!

31 "Therefore a man shall leave his father and mother and hold fast to his wife, and the two shall become one flesh." **32** This mystery is profound, and I am saying that it refers to Christ and the church. **33** However, let each one of you love his wife as himself, and let the wife see that she respects her husband.

In these verses, Paul wraps up his commands for wives and husbands. First, he connects his earlier teaching to the creation account. Then, he connects the institution of marriage in creation to Christ's relationship to the church in redemption. Finally, he leaves his married readers with a word of practical instruction.

"Therefore a man shall leave his father and mother and hold fast to his wife, and the two shall become one flesh" is a quotation from Genesis, a text Jesus also quoted (Gen. 2:24; see also Matt. 19:5). At creation, the Lord instituted marriage as a unique human institution. A man and a woman dissolve their primary allegiance to their parents and create a new family with one another. Through their shared life and exclusive commitment, and especially through their sexual relationship, they "become one flesh." This one-flesh relationship is the basis for Paul's command in Ephesians 5:28–30 telling husbands to love their wives as their own bodies. It's also the basis for all Paul's other instructions about marriage. A husband must give himself in love to his wife and a wife must give herself in submission to her husband because they are no longer simply two individuals; they are joined in one flesh. As modern readers, we should note that Paul's appeal to the creation account situates his teaching about marriage beyond his letter's first-century context. It's not merely the husbands and wives in Ephesus who had to order their relationship this way; it's every married couple since the world was created. When spouses give themselves to one another as Paul commands, they are living according to God's original creation design.

Verse 32 is difficult to parse, and commentators disagree about what "mystery" Paul is referencing. You'll remember from chapter 3 that Paul uses "mystery" to mean a spiritual reality that was once hidden and now has been revealed (vv. 1–6). So, while it's possible that the "mystery" here is marriage, it's hard to see how marriage has the hidden and revealed dynamic. His earlier point, after all, is that God instituted marriage at creation. More probably, Paul is saying that the "mystery" is the relationship between Christ and the church that once was hidden in the marriage relationship but now is revealed in the marriage relationship.[11] In this understanding, marriage is a picture of Christ's relationship to the church. Previously, the spiritual lesson of marriage was hidden. Although there were hints in the prophets' metaphors of a marriage between God and his people (see, for example, Isa. 62:4–5; Ezek. 16), when Old Testament believers looked at married couples, they primarily saw married couples. Now, with the coming of Christ and the institution of the church, believers can look at married couples and see the bigger spiritual realities of the church's union with Christ, Christ's love for the church, and the church's submission to Christ. Any given marriage will do this imperfectly, of course, but marriages are

---

11 O'Brien, *Ephesians*, 431–35.

everywhere, and so observers have scores of opportunities to glimpse these spiritual truths. If you see one portrait of a famous historical person, you'll get one small impression of how he or she looked. If you can survey a whole gallery of portraits of the same person by different artists, you'll have a fuller sense of that subject's true appearance. Every godly marriage is one picture of the self-giving relationship of Christ and the church. If you're married, your marriage serves as an encouragement and lesson to the church: *Look and learn how Christ and the church give themselves for another!* And it serves as an invitation to unbelievers: *Do you want to be loved and cared for like this? Come to Christ and join his church.*

Because of the weighty spiritual realities married couples are displaying to the world, it's all the more important that they would walk carefully in their relationship. And so Paul concludes his teaching by returning to practical commands for ordinary husbands and their ordinary wives. He says to husbands, "Let each one of you love his wife as himself," restating his previous instruction for self-giving love. And to wives, "Let the wife see that she respects her husband," again affirming the wife's call to humbly receive her husband's leadership. In this way, married couples serve one another, honor the Lord, and point to glorious spiritual realities they can only begin to grasp.

Ephesians 6

Stand Firm

¹ Children, obey your parents in the Lord, for this is right.
² "Honor your father and mother" (this is the first commandment with a promise), ³ "that it may go well with you and that you may live long in the land."

If you had the privilege of growing up as a child in the church, you probably remember your excitement when the sermon included a word directly to children. Your ears pricked up as you looked straight at the preacher, eager to hear his next comment. Your friends probably did the same. The fact that the pastor was addressing children gave all children in the congregation a sense of importance. We can imagine that something similar probably happened in Ephesus when Paul's words in verses 1 and 2 were read in the church. First-century children stopped squirming and sat up straight. *The apostle's talking to us!* As with Paul's words to wives (5:22–24, 33), his words to children (and, later, bondservants, 6:5–8) ascribe dignity to an often-disregarded group by affirming their valuable place in the covenant community, calling them to freely obey his command, and elevating their duty to serve others as one aspect of their high calling to serve the Lord. Paul here gives children a command and three reasons to obey it.

The command is as simple to understand as it is difficult to keep: "Children, obey your parents." Paul is speaking to "children," young people who are still in their parents' home. This is a temporary role. In the preceding section, Paul acknowledged that children eventually grow up and generally leave their parents' homes in order to form their own families (5:31). Children love and care for their parents over a lifetime, but, during the limited season when a child is dependent on her parents and under their "discipline and instruction" (6:4), she has a special duty to obey them. She should not only obey them but also "honor" them—do good to them as they fulfill their role as parents. Paul refers to "parents" and to "your father and mother," calling children to give obedience and honor to both parents. He also refers to them as "*your* father and mother," affirming that all adults don't have blanket authority over all children, but only as far as they are each given particular roles that relate to one another.

The first reason children should obey their parents is because they do it "in the Lord." Ultimately, obedience to Mom and Dad is an expression of obedience to God himself. Jesus affirmed that the citizens of his kingdom include children (Matt. 19:13–15). Children can have genuine, saving faith in Christ and changed lives just like believers who are much older. For children, one mark of new life in Christ is obedience to parents. Although it doesn't seem particularly glorious to be told to make your bed, brush your teeth, and sit quietly in church, obeying those commands is part of a higher calling—the highest possible calling!—to serve the Lord. We can encourage children: "That bed you have to make is no ordinary bed but is a bed belonging to the great King of all the universe. He's sent word by two of his other servants—you call them 'Mom' and 'Dad'—to ask you to make it, and he notices and is pleased when you do. It's difficult to make the bed every day, but it's the way you take up your valuable role in the kingdom and honor its King." Obeying parents "in the Lord" also qualifies the limits of obedience. Parents don't have God-given authority to require sin or forbid righteousness; children must obey their parents only as far as the parents' directives serve the ultimate purpose of obeying the Lord.

The second reason for children's obedience is that it's obviously "right." Across eras and cultures—even in communities where the gospel hasn't reached—people generally agree that kids should do what their parents say. If, in modern times and ascendant culture, it's become increasingly popular for parents to defer to their children and for children to rule their families with their emotions and preferences, that should strike us as wrong. One of the obvious marks of mankind's descent into unchecked wickedness is that people become "disobedient to parents" (Rom. 1:30; see also 2 Tim. 3:2).

Not only is obedience to parents generally "right" in human civilization, it's particularly "right" according to Scripture. Paul cites the fifth commandment (Ex. 20:12; Deut. 5:16) as his third reason (and as an incentive) for children's obedience. Similar to when he appealed to the creation account in his teaching on marriage (Eph. 5:31), Paul's appeal to the Ten Commandments demonstrates that his exhortation isn't culturally bound. Children in Old Testament Israel needed to obey their parents; children in first-century Ephesus needed to obey their parents; children around the world today should obey their parents. Additionally, Paul's appeal to the creation institution and the Ten Commandments affirms that both of those foundational texts have enduring implications for Christians' new life in Christ. Paul even nods to the fact that the commandment he cited doesn't exist in isolation: It's just one part of God's moral law summarized in the Ten Commandments ("the first commandment with a promise"). Obeying the fifth commandment—and, by implication, the whole moral law given on Sinai to the people of God—is a continued obligation for God's people today.

Finally, Paul highlights the reward attached to fifth-commandment obedience: "that it may go well with you and that you may live long in the land" (Eph. 6:3; see also Ex. 20:12; Deut. 5:16). We're often quick to clarify that obedience to God's law doesn't secure merit with God. Nothing we do earns our salvation; nothing we fail to do disqualifies us from his love. Thanks be to God! But Paul (and the fifth commandment) *do* teach that obedience to God's law brings blessing. Because God designed the world, it makes sense that things would generally "go well" when we live in it according to his plan. (You're free to drive down the wrong side of the highway, but your trip will go much better if you obey the signs and stay in the correct lane!) What's more, God is pleased when we do what he commands, and, though we never *deserve* his favor, he *freely promises it to us* in response to our obedience. To "live long in the land" has rich meaning throughout the Old Testament that we don't have space to explore here. Simply put, though, it's enjoying God's gracious presence—both in this life and in the life to come. It's not easy for children to obey and honor imperfect parents in all the mundane duties of family life, but God promises he'll be with them and bless them when they do.

⁴ Fathers, do not provoke your children to anger, but bring them up in the discipline and instruction of the Lord.

Parents, too, have a duty before the Lord in their role. Paul specifically addresses "fathers" here, which may be because he wants to highlight fathers' responsibility for training children in the home[1] or because he's using fathers as the representative of both parents.[2] Either way, since he included mothers and fathers in the previous verses, it's logical that there's application for both parents in this one. Many other places in Scripture affirm that mothers, also, ought to discipline and instruct their children (see, for example, Deut. 21:18–19; Prov. 1:8–9; 2 Tim. 1:5). As he's done repeatedly in this letter, Paul gives a prohibition followed by a positive command. Because it's entirely possible to be a Christian parent who doesn't parent Christianly,[3] Paul lays out principles for how we can honor Christ in our parenting.

Paul tells fathers not to "provoke [their] children to anger." Although a father has rightful authority over his own children, he must not abuse it. In chapter 4, Paul cautioned all believers against sinful or prolonged anger and warned that Satan exploits uncontrolled emotions (vv. 26–27). A harsh father—one who

---

1 Peter T. O'Brien, *The Letter to the Ephesians*, The Pillar New Testament Commentary (Eerdmans, 1999), 445.
2 Charles Hodge, *A Commentary on Ephesians*, Geneva Series of Commentaries (1856; repr., Banner of Truth, 2003), 264.
3 I think I heard this phrase somewhere, but I don't recall where.

makes unreasonable demands that his children can't obey or who relates to his children in an unloving way—will not only sin himself but "provoke" his children to lose control of their emotions. Parents must know their own children ("*your* children") and parent according to each son or daughter's maturity, needs, and abilities.

Instead of provoking, fathers are to "discipline and instruct" their children. Fathers are to be neither irritating micromanagers nor absentee parents. They shouldn't aggravate their children, but they should lovingly instruct them. They say "no" to some things and "yes" to others, give consequences for some behaviors and praise for others, shield their children from some influences and diligently expose them to others—but all with the good of their children in mind. They should relate to their children with the same truthfulness, gentleness, generosity, purity, kindness, tenderness, and forgiveness that they owe every other member of the church (see 4:25–32). Children may be young and small, but godly parents ought to treat them with dignity and love.

It's common for parents to want to train their children in their own image—to teach the kids to love the parents' favorite music, sports, food, books, and movies. If the parents prioritize career achievement, they'll want their kids to do so too. If the parents value healthy eating, they'll make that a goal for their kids. Life in Christ, however, means that what's most important to parents is not that their children would become like them but that their children would become like Christ. They train their children "in the discipline and instruction *of the Lord*." They thoroughly prepare their children for life in this world under Christ (even multiplication tables and French verbs serve the Lord when they are learned and used for his glory!). And parents train their children especially in the knowledge of Christ: teaching them the Scriptures, worshiping

God together in their home, and bringing them to worship with the church. Parents are themselves under the Lord, and they "bring [their children] up" in the Lord. In Christ, unreasonable autocrats become tender disciple makers.

⁵ Bondservants, obey your earthly masters with fear and trembling, with a sincere heart, as you would Christ, ⁶ not by the way of eye-service, as people-pleasers, but as bondservants of Christ, doing the will of God from the heart, ⁷ rendering service with a good will as to the Lord and not to man, ⁸ knowing that whatever good anyone does, this he will receive back from the Lord, whether he is a bondservant or is free.

Paul now turns to his final pair of roles: bondservants and masters. Slavery was a common institution in the first century, and, by some estimates, 10 to 20 percent of people in the Roman Empire were enslaved (or "bondservants").[4] This means the bondservant-master relationship characterized a significant portion of all labor relationships. These roles also had some fluidity. In the Roman system, enslaved people could be released and reenter society as free laborers, and poor people could sell themselves into slavery to gain a more stable life.[5] Some slaves were even considered part of a master's household and participated in the daily life of the home. Although

---

4   "Slavery in Ancient Rome," The British Museum, accessed March 19, 2025, https://www .britishmuseum.org/.

5   Peter Temin, "The Labor Supply of the Early Roman Empire," Massachusetts Institute of Technology Department of Economics Work Paper Series, November 2001, 2–3, 8, 12, https://economics.mit.edu/sites/default/files/2022-08/The%20Labor%20Supply%20of%20 the%20Early%20Roman%20Empire.pdf.

"bondservants" and "masters" may seem like foreign categories, Paul's instructions have application for modern readers in the workplace. Whether believers are in authority or under authority at work, we must honor the Lord. In these verses, Paul gives bondservants a command, explains how they ought to obey this command, and holds out an incentive from the Lord for their obedience.

Before we consider the command in these verses, though, let's examine whether Paul is implicitly condoning slavery. Modern readers are often puzzled about why Paul would give instructions to bondservants and masters rather than calling for slavery's abolition. This is an important question, and others have written extensively about it.[6] For our purposes, let's briefly note four truths. First, we need to make sure we aren't resisting the mere existence of authoritative and submissive roles. The Bible affirms that all people have equal dignity and value before God, but it also sets those same people *in* authority in some circumstances and *under* authority in others.[7] For example, a child submits to her parents; both children and parents submit to the civil government; children, parents, and civil magistrates all submit to the Lord. In different spheres—including the workplace—some people are in authority and others are under authority. The fact that one person would work for another person and that the employer would have the authority to dictate the terms of the employee's work isn't inherently wrong. It's also not wrong if the employee's labor brings profit to the employer.

---

6   See, for example, John Murray, "The Ordinance of Labor," chap. 4 in *Principles of Conduct: Aspects of Biblical Ethics* (Eerdmans, 1957), 82–106.

7   For example, the Westminster Shorter Catechism, q. and a. 64, says the fifth commandment requires "preserving the honor and performing the duties, belonging to every one in their several places and relations, as superiors, inferiors, or equals." Westminster Shorter Catechism, *The Westminster Confession of Faith: Together with the Larger Catechism and the Shorter Catechism with Scripture Proofs*, 3rd ed. (Christian Education and Publications, 1990), 21.

Second, though working under someone's authority and for their financial gain isn't in itself sinful, Scripture does explicitly prohibit the grievous harms that often accompany slavery. Manstealing (Ex. 21:16; Deut. 24:7; 1 Tim. 1:10), killing and bodily injury (Ex. 20:13; Rom. 13:9), rape and sexual abuse (Deut. 22:23–29; Eph. 5:3–5), and refusing to pay a worker wages (Rom. 4:4; 1 Tim. 5:18; James 5:4) are all condemned in the Bible's teaching, including in Paul's own writing. The abusive practices of race-based, chattel slavery (the slavery once widely practiced in the United States), for example, are incompatible with life in Christ.

Third, in each set of instructions in this section of his letter (5:22–6:9), Paul's objective isn't encouraging people to participate in a particular institution but teaching them how to live if that's where God has put them for a time. Paul isn't urging people to get married or to have children, nor is he championing slavery. There's a biblical case for getting married and having children if the Lord providentially allows, just as there's a biblical argument for abolishing slavery—but that's not Paul's point here. Instead, he's looking at the roles the Ephesians are currently occupying and teaching the believers how to honor God in those situations. We should always read a text in view of the author's objective. It's not fair to complain that a writer fails to make a particular argument when his aim is to make a different one.

Fourth, though it's not the point of Paul's writing in Ephesians 6 to comment on the morality of slaveholding, his description of the bondservant-master relationship does influence what we think about slavery. If the Ephesian church took Paul's commands to heart, the institution of slavery would be so totally upended that, among Christians at least, it couldn't easily continue. (And, indeed, in the history of the world, where Christianity has gone, slavery has eventually receded.)[8] Just as his explanation of husbands and wives as a picture of Christ and church makes us favorable to the possibility of getting married, Paul's radical vision for the flourishing of bondservants and masters makes us disinclined to tolerate slavery.

Before looking at the specifics of this text, we should note one final thing: As with Paul's earlier instructions to wives and children, his words in these verses give dignity to a group often demeaned in first-century society. He affirms bondservants' rightful place in the assembly of God's people, acknowledges they have the ability to freely obey, and elevates their duty to their masters as one aspect of their greater calling to serve the Lord God. What's more, when Paul calls them "bondservants of Christ," we remember how he earlier called himself a "prisoner of Christ" (3:1). In Christ, apostles and slaves are in the same position: at the disposal of Christ. Everything Paul says in 6:5–9 lifts bondservants up in the hearing of the church as precious to the Lord.

Paul's basic command is brief: "Obey your earthly masters." In the workplace, those *under* authority should do what those *in* authority ask them to do. By identifying the authorities as "earthly masters," though, Paul sets a mundane command in a glorious context. Bondservants may be at the beck and call of an imperfect master, but they ultimately serve Christ ("as you would Christ" and "as to the Lord and not to man"). Bondservants may do ordinary tasks, but they do them as "bondservants of Christ" who are "doing the will of God from the heart." And bondservants may or may not receive fair wages or work under ideal terms ("whether he is a bondservant or is free"), but they "receive back from the Lord" for

---

8   Sharon James, *Is Christianity Good for the World?*, TGC Hard Questions (Crossway, 2023), 4–14.

their obedient labor. Daily labor is never merely daily labor when it's done "to the Lord." As we saw with the other pairs in this section of Ephesians (5:22–6:9), Christ's ultimate authority also limits earthly authority. No master has God-given authority to require a bondservant to sin or forbid her from righteous acts. She must obey her earthly master only as far as his demands accord with the heavenly master's.

Ultimate obedience to a heavenly master has sweeping implications for how bondservants obey earthly masters. They must obey "with fear and trembling," not making fun or being critical of the master, but having respect for his authority in the workplace. They obey "with a sincere heart," not working with one hand and tearing down with the other, but doing tasks wholeheartedly for the master's interests. They also obey conscientiously, whether or not the master even notices, "not by the way of eye-service, as people-pleasers, but as bondservants of Christ, doing the will of God from the heart." And they obey cheerfully, "rendering service with a good will," as those who are eager to serve the master so they can serve Christ.

Paul's final phrase "whether he is a bondservant or is free" broadens his command to all kinds of workers in all kinds of workplaces. Regardless of the specifics of your work arrangement—whether you are paid much or little, have a kind boss or an overbearing one, work only in your home or for someone outside it—you work "as to the Lord." The labor of a CEO in a gleaming downtown office building is neither more nor less valuable to the Lord than the labor of a housekeeper in a struggling small-town motel.

These verses also contain an incentive. The Lord is pleased with our faithful service in all kinds of work arrangements, promising that we will "receive [good] back from the Lord" when we do good to others. As we saw in our discussion of verse 2, our obedience to the Lord doesn't *deserve* God's favor or *earn* anything from the Lord, but he kindly says he'll reward us when we obey. Because God designed the world and knows best how it should operate, it makes sense to conduct ourselves at work according to his direction. What's more, Scripture acknowledges a judgment from God "according to . . . works" (Rom. 2:6; see also 1 Pet. 1:17).[9] The work of the poorest slave comes before the Lord for scrutiny, as does the work of the wealthiest business owner. And God does good to each in response to obedience to him. "Whatever good . . . , this he will receive back" has the sense of a return in kind—as we are gracious to others in the workplace, the Lord is gracious to us; as we are generous, the Lord is generous; as we forgive, the Lord assures us of his forgiveness. Although you may work a lifetime without a bonus or raise or "good job!" from your employer, the Lord never

---

9   John Stott explains Rom. 2:6 this way: "[Paul] is affirming that, although justification is indeed by faith, judgment will be according to works. The reason for this is not hard to find. It is that the day of judgment will be a public occasion. Its purpose will be less to determine God's judgment than to announce and vindicate it. . . . Such a public occasion, on which a public verdict will be given and a public sentence passed, will require public and verifiable evidence to support them. And the only public evidence available will be our works, what we have done and have been seen to do. The presence or absence of saving faith in our hearts will be disclosed by the presence or absence of good works of love in our lives. The apostles Paul and James both teach this same truth, that authentic saving faith invariably issues in good works, and that if it does not, it is bogus, even dead." John Stott, *Romans: God's Good News for the World* (InterVarsity Press, 1994), 83–84. Also, the Westminster Confession of Faith explains that believers' good works do not come from their own ability, are not perfect, and do not merit salvation, yet "the persons of believers being accepted through Christ, their good works are also accepted in Him; not as though they were in this life wholly unblameable and unreprovable in God's sight; but that He, looking upon them in His Son, is pleased to accept and reward that which is sincere, although accompanied with many weaknesses and imperfections." Westminster Confession of Faith, in *The Westminster Confession of Faith: Together with the Larger Catechism and the Shorter Catechism with Scripture Proofs*, 3rd ed. (Christian Education and Publications, 1990), 16.6 (p. 52); see also 16.1–5 (pp. 49–52).

overlooks service done for his glory, and he promises to bless you.[10] In Christ, half-hearted workers become wholehearted.

⁹ Masters, do the same to them, and stop your threatening, knowing that he who is both their Master and yours is in heaven, and that there is no partiality with him.

Paul's instructions to masters, "do the same to them," refers masters back to his previous commands to bondservants (vv. 5–8). In Christ, what's right for a bondservant is right for a master. If bondservants are to be respectful to their masters, then masters ought to treat their bondservants with respect and dignity. If bondservants are to work sincerely without a hidden agenda, masters should deal honestly with their bondservants and not manipulate them. If bondservants are to conscientiously serve the Lord in their labor, whether or not anyone notices, masters shouldn't treat their bondservants one way when others are looking and another behind closed doors. If bondservants are to work cheerfully and eagerly for their masters, masters should be joyful and encouraging as they interact with their bondservants. And if bondservants are to willingly obey their masters' commands, masters should "stop [their] threatening" and instead direct their bondservants reasonably.

The grounds for this radical equivalence become clear in Paul's next phrases: "knowing that he who is both their Master and yours is in heaven, and that there is no partiality with him." Why should bondservants and masters conduct themselves according to

---

10 Westminster Confession of Faith, 16.6.

the same standards and treat one another with the same dignity? Because God in heaven has authority over both of them, and "there is no partiality with him." God's righteous requirement is not a sliding scale, depending on whether a person is rich or poor, young or old, male or female, in authority or under authority. We must all live as those who are in Christ. Throughout his instructions for our relationships at home and work, Paul has emphasized the same themes: We seek the Lord's help to walk in our new spiritual life, humbly serve him in the roles he's given us for today, and "[submit] to one another out of reverence for Christ" (5:21). In Christ, harsh taskmasters become kind employers.

EPHESIANS 6:10–13

[10] Finally, be strong in the Lord and in the strength of his might. [11] Put on the whole armor of God, that you may be able to stand against the schemes of the devil. [12] For we do not wrestle against flesh and blood, but against the rulers, against the authorities, against the cosmic powers over this present darkness, against the spiritual forces of evil in the heavenly places. [13] Therefore take up the whole armor of God, that you may be able to withstand in the evil day, and having done all, to stand firm.

In John Bunyan's famous allegory, *The Pilgrim's Progress*, Christian set out on a pilgrimage to the Celestial City. Early in his journey, he came to the Palace Beautiful, where the gracious daughters of the house welcomed Christian to a meal. Bunyan wrote, "Now the table was furnished with fat things, and with wine that was well refined: and all their talk at the table was about the Lord of the hill; as, namely, about what he had done, and wherefore he did what he did, and why he had built that house."[11] But, as much as he might have liked to, Christian wasn't permitted to stay permanently at the palace, talking about the Lord and his work. After a few days' rest, the daughters took him to the armory and dressed him in a full suit of armor. They knew what Christian didn't: As soon as he reached the next valley, he'd have to face the evil dragon, Apollyon.

So far in this letter, Paul has spread a feast for the Ephesians. He's welcomed them to meditate on the knowledge of Christ and the joy of belonging to his church (see, for example, 3:14–21). He's shown them how far they've already come in their pilgrimage and encouraged them with the greatness of Christ's love for them (see, for example, 2:1–10). He's even given them glimpses of the future glories that await (see, for example, 1:11–14). But he doesn't permit them to stay at this table forever. Evil forces are at work in the world, and, though the Ephesians don't yet realize it, they need to prepare for battle.

In these verses, Paul gives the church a reason for courage, explains the war we're fighting, and tells us what we'll need to win. "Finally," Paul writes, "be strong in the Lord and in the strength of his might." Although he's about to reveal some terrifying truths about a powerful enemy who is out to get us, he begins with a reason for courage. We can be strong "in the Lord" and have the strength "of his might." The same Christ who rescued us from sin and Satan when he saved us (2:1–10) will give us strength against those evil powers now. Like a mother preparing her young children

---

11 John Bunyan, *Pilgrim's Progress from This World to That Which Is to Come*, in *The Works of John Bunyan with an Introduction to Each Treatise, Notes, and a Sketch of His Life, Times, and Contemporaries*, vol. 3 *Allegorical, Figurative, and Symbolical*, ed. George Offor (1854; repr., Banner of Truth, 1999), 109.

for a scary new experience, the Lord assures us he's been there before and will be with us every moment as we go.

Next, Paul surveys the battle we're entering. Because Christ's church is the visible expression of his glory and his kingdom, Satan would like nothing more than to destroy it. "The schemes of the devil" are his plans to bring down the church by any means possible. Wherever he can, he'll tempt believers to sin (Gen. 4:7; Eph. 4:27), sow doubts about God (Gen. 3:4–5), speak lies about God's word (John 8:44; Rev. 12:9), and create division among God's people (2 Cor. 2:10–11). Lest the Ephesians dismiss this spiritual danger as inconsequential because it's invisible, Paul assures them the threat is real. "We do not wrestle against flesh and blood," he writes, "but against the rulers, . . . authorities, . . . cosmic powers over this present darkness, . . . [and] spiritual forces of evil." Each of these terms reminds us not to underestimate the enemy of God's people. Satan and his angels are powerful, and they have real authority. Yes, the devil is bound and ultimately subject to God (Rev. 20:2; see also Job 1:6–12), but he's still dangerous. Just because that snarling dog is on a chain doesn't mean you should try to pet him. And if you have to walk through his yard, you need a clear strategy.

Paul then tells us what we'll need in order to win our fight against Satan: "the whole armor of God." In the coming verses, he'll explain the parts of the armor and show us how to suit up for battle. In these verses, he simply tells us that the armor comes from God and promises us that it's exactly what we need. Paul begins with a reason for courage, and he ends with a reason for courage. When we take up the armor God provides, we will "be able to withstand in the evil day, and having done all, to stand firm." When the "evil day" of battle ends at Jesus's return, the church will be in the same position we were when it began—safely united to Christ. Believers have an advantage that no army in the history of warfare has ever had: We know from the beginning that we will surely win. Satan is a very real enemy, but God is our "very present help" (Ps. 46:1). "Thanks be to God, who gives us the victory through our Lord Jesus Christ" (1 Cor. 15:57)!

EPHESIANS 6:14

¹⁴ Stand therefore, having fastened on the belt of truth, and having put on the breastplate of righteousness,

If you've ever been to a war museum in a country with a long history, you may have seen rooms filled with armor. You probably noticed that Japanese Samurai armor was different from armor in Renaissance France because the soldiers who wore each type were fighting different wars. So, too, the armor of God is carefully designed with the "schemes of the devil" (v. 11) in view. A spiritual war requires specialized spiritual equipment. Another thing you may have noted is that armor distinguished one side from another. On the battlefield, a soldier could spot combatants wearing a familiar crest or carrying a certain shield and recognize his own unit. Although we may be accustomed to thinking of this well-known passage (vv. 10–20) in terms of individual Christians, Paul is describing the armor of an entire army: the church of Christ. We fight Satan together, equipped with the same spiritual weapons. One more lesson of an armor display is that those intricate suits are useless standing on their museum pedestals. The true value of armor is when it's actually worn by a soldier in battle. So, too, we must actively put on the armor of God. Throughout verses 10–20,

Paul uses a variety of words to describe how we suit up: "put on" (vv. 11, 14, 15), "fastened on" (v. 14), and "take" or "take up" (vv. 13, 16, 17). God provides the armor, and each of these phrases reinforces the idea that we must *use* it.

The first piece of armor in verse 14 is "the belt of truth." In the first-century Roman Empire, a soldier's thick leather belt protected his lower body and kept his robes tucked up and away from his feet.[12] The belt wasn't technically a piece of armor but was the armor's foundational undergarment. For believers, God's word ("truth") is our first and most basic equipment. Satan's earliest tactic ("Did God actually say . . . ?," Gen. 3:1) continues to be one of his strongest. But as we learn the Scriptures, love the Scriptures, and obey the Scriptures—both as individuals and as the church— we prepare ourselves with truth and live according to the truth in order to "stand" (Eph. 6:14) against that great deceiver, Satan (John 8:44; Rev. 12:9).

The second piece of armor in this passage is "the breastplate of righteousness." A Roman soldier's breastplate was a shield that covered the upper half of his body and protected most of his vital organs.[13] Here, "righteousness" may refer to Christ's righteousness, imputed to believers for their justification. This allows us to stand holy before God, impervious to any charges brought against us by the accuser, Satan (Rom. 8:31–35; Rev. 12:10). "Righteousness" could also refer to believers' right conduct—killing sin and walking in holiness as a fruit of God's sanctification in our lives.[14] This protects us from giving "opportunity to the devil" (Eph. 4:27), who crouches at our door in order to tempt us to sin (Gen. 4:7).

---

12 Andrew T. Lincoln, *Ephesians*, Biblical Word Commentary (Word Books, 1990), 447–48.

13 Stott, *Message of Ephesians*, 278.

14 Stott, *Message of Ephesians*, 278–79.

EPHESIANS 6:15

¹⁵ and, as shoes for your feet, having put on the readiness given by the gospel of peace.

The third piece of armor is "shoes" that are "the readiness given by the gospel of peace." A Roman soldier's boots equipped him to march.[15] Here, Paul seems to be nodding to Isaiah's words:

> How beautiful upon the mountains
>   are the feet of him who brings good news,
> who publishes peace, who brings good news of happiness,
>   who publishes salvation,
>   who says to Zion, "Your God reigns." (Isa. 52:7)

Believers—as individuals and as the church—are always ready to proclaim the peace that comes from being reconciled to God in Christ. Wherever we go on our long march through life, we take this good news with us. We must be ready with the gospel because Satan is the great dragon and the expert thief who is poised to snatch away all hope of salvation in Christ (Rev. 12:1–6; see also John 10:10).

EPHESIANS 6:16

¹⁶ In all circumstances take up the shield of faith, with which you can extinguish all the flaming darts of the evil one;

The fourth piece of armor is the "shield of faith." A Roman soldier's shield, like the word for "door" for which it was named, was wide

---

15 Frank Thielman, *Ephesians*, Baker Exegetical Commentary on the New Testament (Baker Academic, 2010), 426.

and tall to cover most of his body.[16] Our "faith" is our complete trust in Christ. Utter neediness might not seem like the best weapon for a battle, but utter neediness that knows where to go for help "in all circumstances" is actually a formidable strength. As we continually look to Christ to supply all we need, we rebuff the "flaming darts of the evil one," who loves to kill and destroy with doubt and temptation (Matt. 10:28–31). As we stand "firm in [our] faith," we resist the devil who "prowls around like a roaring lion, seeking someone to devour" (1 Pet. 5:8–9).

EPHESIANS 6:17

[17] and take the helmet of salvation, and the sword of the Spirit, which is the word of God,

The fifth piece of armor is the "helmet of salvation." A Roman soldier's helmet was both protective (made out of strong metal) and ornamental (decorated with feathers or crests).[17] For believers, meditating on our salvation and praising God for it—what Paul has been doing for much of this letter!—strengthens us in battle. As Charles Hodge wrote, "That which adorns and protects the Christian, which enables him to hold up his head with confidence and joy, is the fact that he is saved."[18] When Satan tried to destroy Job by taking all his earthly comforts, Job resisted him with utter confidence in his salvation:

> For I know that my Redeemer lives,
> and at the last he will stand upon the earth.

---

16 Hodge, *Ephesians*, 284.
17 Stott, *Message of Ephesians*, 281.
18 Hodge, *Ephesians*, 286.

And after my skin has been thus destroyed,
> yet in my flesh I shall see God. (Job 19:25–26)

The sixth piece of armor in Paul's description is the "sword of the Spirit, which is the word of God." A Roman soldier's sword allowed him to both defend himself and attack his enemy. Believers take up the sword when we memorize and study the Bible and seek the Spirit's help to understand and apply it. As a church, hearing the reading and preaching of God's word in the power of the Spirit especially equips us to resist Satan's attacks. When Jesus met Satan's temptations in the wilderness, "It is written" became his constant refrain as he countered Satan's schemes with God's own word (Matt. 4:4, 6, 10). Our enemy is powerful, but we fight with confidence. As Scripture itself promises, when we "resist the devil, . . . he will flee" (James 4:7).

EPHESIANS 6:18–20

18 praying at all times in the Spirit, with all prayer and supplication. To that end, keep alert with all perseverance, making supplication for all the saints, **19** and also for me, that words may be given to me in opening my mouth boldly to proclaim the mystery of the gospel, **20** for which I am an ambassador in chains, that I may declare it boldly, as I ought to speak.

In most depictions of war, prayer is a soldier's last resort—a desperate plea to a distant God when every other option has been tried. We even have a phrase, "foxhole prayers," to mean the kind of prayers offered in the trenches of battle when death and defeat are imminent. Only after the soldier has thrown his last grenade, fired his last bullet, and drained the last drop of water from his canteen does he look heavenward for help. The prayer described in Ephesians 6 couldn't be more different. It's urgent wartime prayer, for sure, but it rises continually from every corner of the battlefield, upholds every soldier, and is the means by which the whole army triumphs.

Following his description of the church's spiritual armor, Paul encourages the Ephesians to fight with prayer. Prayer is not exactly a piece of armor, but it animates the entire battle plan. As with verses 10–17, we may be accustomed to thinking of these verses in individual terms, but we should remember that Paul is speaking to the whole congregation in Ephesus. Prayer is certainly something Christians should do individually, but it's also a vital task for the whole church. We are an army, and the prayer we pray together in corporate worship and prayer meetings is an act of war. By it, we call on God to supply all we need, advance his kingdom, and defeat all his and our enemies. Like the church in Acts, our congregations today must "[devote] themselves to . . . the prayers" (Acts 2:42).

Verse 18 emphasizes how pervasive prayer ought to be in the lives of believers, using the word "all" to describe four characteristics of prayer. (1) We ought to pray "at all times"—in the church, with our families, on our own, among our friends, before a meal, at bedtime, in the morning, as we travel, and with a coworker on the phone. We ought to pray out loud, silently, expansively, quickly, on a schedule, and in response to urgent needs. Rather than viewing prayer as a last resort, we ought to seek out all kinds of opportunities to pray. Such prayer is "in the Spirit"—it's prompted and helped by him (see Rom. 8:26–27). (2) What's more, we ought to offer "all prayer and supplication." Every kind of prayer in Scripture is a kind of prayer we should pray: praise to God, confession of sin, thanksgiving for God's mercies, petitions for big kingdom concerns, and petitions for small daily needs. (3) As we pray, we must "keep alert with all perseverance." Prayer may be a vital spiritual weapon, but it's hard to wield. We rarely see immediate answers and often see nothing at all. The evil one would like to convince us to stop altogether. Like Christ's disciples in Gethsemane, we must "watch and pray" persistently so we aren't vulnerable to Satan's attacks (Matt. 26:41). (4) Finally, we make "supplication for all the saints"—praying for all believers. This includes praying for specific temporal needs like healing and financial provision, but, in the context of spiritual war, it especially means praying for the Lord to strengthen and equip his people and give them victory over sin and Satan. These wartime prayers—at all times, of all kinds, with all our hearts, for all God's people—are prayers the Lord loves to hear and answer. By them, he gives us the victory.

Paul then moves from all-encompassing prayer to a specific request for prayer for himself. He may have been the great apostle, but he was as completely dependent on the Lord as any member of the Ephesian congregation. By his request, he reminds us that we should both pray for others ("for all the saints") and ask others to pray for us ("and also for me"). Paul asks the church to pray for him to be clear and bold as he preaches the gospel. As John Stott writes, "Some preachers have the gift of lucid teaching, but their sermons lack solid content; their substance has become diluted by fear. Others are bold as lions. They fear nobody and omit nothing. But what they say is confused and confusing."[19]

---

19 Stott, *Message of Ephesians*, 286.

Paul recognizes these temptations and asks the Ephesians to pray that he would clearly explain the deep truths of the gospel, "that words may be given to me in opening my mouth boldly to proclaim the mystery of the gospel." Next, he asks them to pray for him to preach with courage and power: "that I may declare it boldly, as I ought to speak." From a human perspective, everything is working against Paul, "an ambassador in chains," being an effective preacher. But Paul knows that though he's bound, the "word of God is not bound!" (2 Tim. 2:9). The ministry of even an imprisoned preacher can call people to Christ. And so Paul asks for help in the only place he's sure to get it: from the hand of God by the prayers of the saints.

²¹ So that you also may know how I am and what I am doing, Tychicus the beloved brother and faithful minister in the Lord will tell you everything. ²² I have sent him to you for this very purpose, that you may know how we are, and that he may encourage your hearts.

At first glance, the substance of these verses is simple: Paul sends Tychicus from Rome to Ephesus with news and encouragement. Tychicus is a "beloved brother and faithful minister in the Lord," a companion and fellow worker with Paul. Luke describes Tychicus and another believer, Trophimus, as "Asians" (Acts 20:4). Later, Luke specifies that Trophimus is "Ephesian" (Acts 21:29), and so, by implication, Tychicus may be Ephesian too.[20] But

---

20 Stott, *Message of Ephesians*, 288.

whether or not he's from Ephesus, Tychicus is from the same region as Ephesus, has been with Paul in Rome, and now is headed back, probably with this letter in his hand. Tychicus also brings a report about the church in Rome ("how we are") and words of exhortation and encouragement from Paul ("so that you also may know how I am and what I am doing, . . . [he] will tell you everything"). On the surface, these verses seem like a basic travel itinerary.

But in a letter to the church largely about life together in Christ, Paul's brief words here affirm the value of communication and cooperation between local churches. Paul wanted the church in Ephesus to know how the church in Rome was doing, and, in view of his exhortation to pray "for all the saints" (v. 18), we can assume he intended the Ephesians to turn news into supplication. So, too, our churches ought to have real concern for God's work in other congregations. As we have opportunity, we should update other churches in our community and in our denomination about how our church is and what it is doing. And we should receive reports from other churches with genuine interest and a commitment to prayer.

Paul didn't only send news to Ephesus; he sent a person. Paul willingly gave up "beloved" and "faithful" Tychicus "for this very purpose," that Tychicus could "encourage [the Ephesians'] hearts," likely with his gospel ministry. We too should hold our church members loosely—perhaps especially our most gifted and beloved members!—looking for opportunities to share them with other congregations for the church's good. The Lord may call our church to release a group of members to start a new church in another community, loan our pastor to fill a pulpit or provide oversight to a struggling church in another town, or send members to proclaim

Christ on the foreign mission field. This is painful. It's also precious to Christ who "gave himself up" (5:25) for the church.

23 Peace be to the brothers, and love with faith, from God the Father and the Lord Jesus Christ. **24** Grace be with all who love our Lord Jesus Christ with love incorruptible.

We've already read two prayers of Paul for the Ephesians (1:15–23; 3:14–21), but he can't close out his letter to them without one more. In these benediction verses, he returns to many of the themes of his letter and prays that believers will experience them in their lives. Earlier, Paul proclaimed the peace believers have with God (2:1–10) and with one another (2:11–22). The church is one body united to one Lord (4:1–16). Here, then, he asks God to grant "peace . . . to the brothers." Earlier, Paul explored the depths of Christ's love for the believers—love even beyond their ability to comprehend (3:14–19). He also exhorted the congregation members to love one another in scores of practical ways (4:25–32; 5:1–6:9). Here, then, he identifies the believers as those who "love our Lord Jesus Christ" and asks God to give them "love with faith." Earlier, Paul repeatedly pointed to grace as the sole source of every spiritual blessing (1:3–14; 2:4, 5, 8; 3:2, 8). Here, he asks the Lord for his "grace [to] be with" them.

Above all, Paul points to Christ. At the beginning of the letter, he introduced himself as "an apostle of Christ Jesus" (1:1), and so he proves to be. In the course of six chapters, he has savored Christ's redemption of his people, praised him for his heavenly rule, celebrated his work in gathering and uniting and perfecting his church, meditated on his love, and taught us about new life in him. Here, his final words remind the church that loving Christ is the sum of our identity. Yes, we are Jews and Gentiles and wives and husbands and children and parents and bondservants and masters. Yes, we are alive and are light and are soldiers in a cosmic spiritual war. But, in the end, the most important thing that could ever be said of us is this: We are those "who love our Lord Jesus Christ with love incorruptible."

Recommended Resources

Brownback, Lydia. *Ephesians: Growing in Christ*. Flourish Bible Study. Crossway, 2023.

If you'd like to study Ephesians on your own or in a group, this ten-week Bible study workbook is a useful resource. It includes background information for the book and questions to help readers understand, discuss, and apply the text.

Carson, D. A. *Praying with Paul: A Call to Spiritual Reformation.* Baker Academic, 2015.

This volume (formerly titled *A Call to Spiritual Reformation: Priorities from Paul and His Prayers*) examines the New Testament prayers of Paul, including the two in Ephesians. Carson's commentary is rich and practical, emphasizing how Paul's prayers can shape our own.

Hill, Robert. Ephesians Sermon Series. Preached at Pinehaven Presbyterian Church in Clinton, Mississippi. November 2013–March 2015. https://www.sermonaudio.com/series/46572.

I learned to study Paul's book about Christ and his church in the context of the church. This sermon series, preached by my own pastor in my own local congregation, stirred my heart to love Christ's body and, years later, helped me write this volume. Listen to these recordings if you like, but, better yet, commit to showing up in your own church and hearing your own pastor preach. That's where you'll grow in the knowledge of Christ and experience the fullness of Christ—the one who fills all in all.

Stott, John R. W. *The Message of Ephesians*. The Bible Speaks Today. Revised Edition. IVP Academic, 2021.
This accessible commentary on Ephesians will help you continue learning about Paul's letter and how it applies to the lives of believers today. John Stott's verse-by-verse explanation of the text is thorough and also thoroughly readable.

Timelines and Maps

Timeline of Paul's Ministry[1]

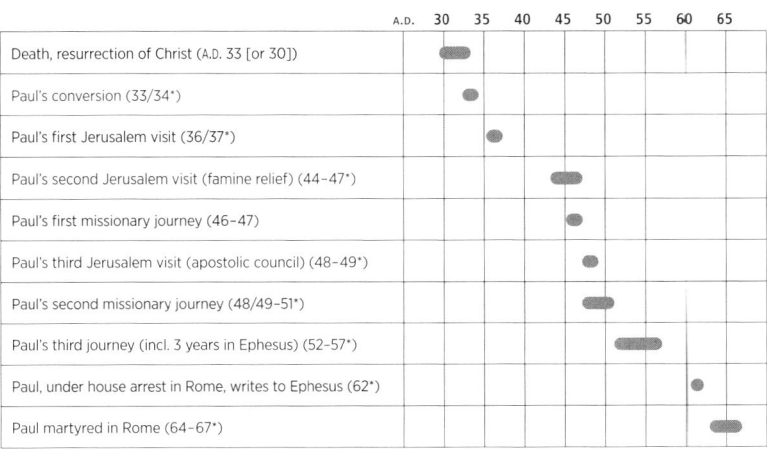

	A.D.	30	35	40	45	50	55	60	65
Death, resurrection of Christ (A.D. 33 [or 30])		●●							
Paul's conversion (33/34*)		●							
Paul's first Jerusalem visit (36/37*)			●						
Paul's second Jerusalem visit (famine relief) (44–47*)					●●				
Paul's first missionary journey (46–47)					●				
Paul's third Jerusalem visit (apostolic council) (48–49*)						●			
Paul's second missionary journey (48/49–51*)						●●			
Paul's third journey (incl. 3 years in Ephesus) (52–57*)							●●		
Paul, under house arrest in Rome, writes to Ephesus (62*)								●	
Paul martyred in Rome (64–67*)									●●

denotes approximate date; / signifies either/or

1 Timeline adapted from the *ESV Study Bible*, ed. Lane Dennis et al. (Crossway, 2009), 2258.

Major Events in the Life of Paul[2]

AD 5–10?   Born in Tarsus, an Israelite from the tribe of Benjamin and a Roman citizen (Acts 22:3, 28; Rom. 11:1; Phil. 3:5); raised in either Jerusalem (Acts 22:3?) or Tarsus

15–20?   Trained as a Pharisee by Gamaliel I (Acts 22:3; 26:5; Gal. 1:14; Phil. 3:5–6)

33*   Death, resurrection of Christ

33*   Present at Stephen's stoning; persecuted Christians (Acts 7:58; 8:1; 22:4; 26:9–11; 1 Cor. 15:9; Gal. 1:13; Phil. 3:6)

33*   **Converted, called, and commissioned on the way to Damascus** (Acts 9:1–19; 22:6–11; 26:12–18; Gal. 1:15–16)

34–37*   Stayed in Damascus a short time (Acts 9:19); left for Arabia (2 Cor. 11:32; Gal. 1:17); returned to Damascus (Gal. 1:17; Acts 9:19–22?); escaped through city wall to avoid arrest (Acts 9:23–25; 2 Cor. 11:32–33)

36/37*   **Met with Peter, saw James, in Jerusalem** (Acts 9:26–30; Gal. 1:18–19); Hellenists sought to kill him; fled to Tarsus (Acts 9:28–30; Gal. 1:21)

37–45   Ministered in Syria/Cilicia (2 Cor. 11:22–27?; Gal. 1:21)

44–47*   Ministered with Barnabas in Antioch (Acts 11:25–26); **Second Visit to Jerusalem;** time of famine (Acts 11:27–30; Gal. 2:1–10)

46–47   **First Missionary Journey** (Acts 13:4–14:26): 1.5 years?

48*   With Barnabas, spent "no little time" in Antioch (Acts 14:28; Gal. 2:11–14); wrote Galatians

48–49*   **Returned to Jerusalem for the apostolic council** (Acts 15:1–29); Paul and Barnabas returned to Antioch (Acts 15:30–33), but dispute over John Mark caused them to part ways (Acts 15:36–41)

48/49–51*   **Second Missionary Journey** (Acts 15:36–18:22): 2.5 years?

---

2   Timeline adapted from *ESV Study Bible*, 2100.

49	Paul and Silas traveled to southern Galatia through Asia Minor, on to Macedonia (Philippi [1 Thess. 2:2], Thessalonica [1 Thess. 2:2; Phil. 4:15–16], and Berea [Acts 17:10–15]), and then to Achaia (Athens [1 Thess. 3:1] and Corinth [2 Cor. 11:7–9])
49–51*	Spent 1.5 years in Corinth (Acts 18:11); appeared before Gallio (Acts 18:12–17); wrote 1 and 2 Thessalonians
51	Returned to Jerusalem? (Acts 18:22)
52–57*	**Third Missionary Journey** (Acts 18:23–21:17): 5 years?
52	Traveled to Antioch, spent "some time"; traveled through Galatia and Phrygia (Acts 18:23)
52–55	Arrived in Ephesus (Acts 19:1; 1 Cor. 16:8); ministered for three years (Acts 20:31) and wrote 1 Corinthians; made brief, "painful visit" to Corinth (2 Cor. 2:1), then returned to Ephesus and wrote severe letter (now lost) to Corinth (2 Cor. 2:3–4; 7:8–16)
55–56*	Traveled north to Macedonia, met Titus (Acts 20:1; 2 Cor. 2:12–13); wrote 2 Corinthians
57*	Wintered in Corinth (Acts 20:2–3; 2 Cor. 9:4), wrote to the Romans from Corinth; traveled to Jerusalem; was arrested (Acts 21:27–36)
57–59	Transferred as prisoner to Caesarea, stayed for two years (Acts 24:27)
60*	Voyaged to Rome; shipwrecked, spent three months on Malta (Acts 28:11); finally arrived in Rome
62*	Under house arrest in Rome (Acts 28:30–31), wrote Ephesians, Philippians, Colossians, Philemon
62–67	Released from house arrest in Rome, travels to Spain (?), wrote 1 Timothy (from Macedonia?) and Titus (from Nicopolis); was rearrested, wrote 2 Timothy from Rome, was martyred

* denotes approximate date; / signifies either/or

The Setting of Ephesians[3]

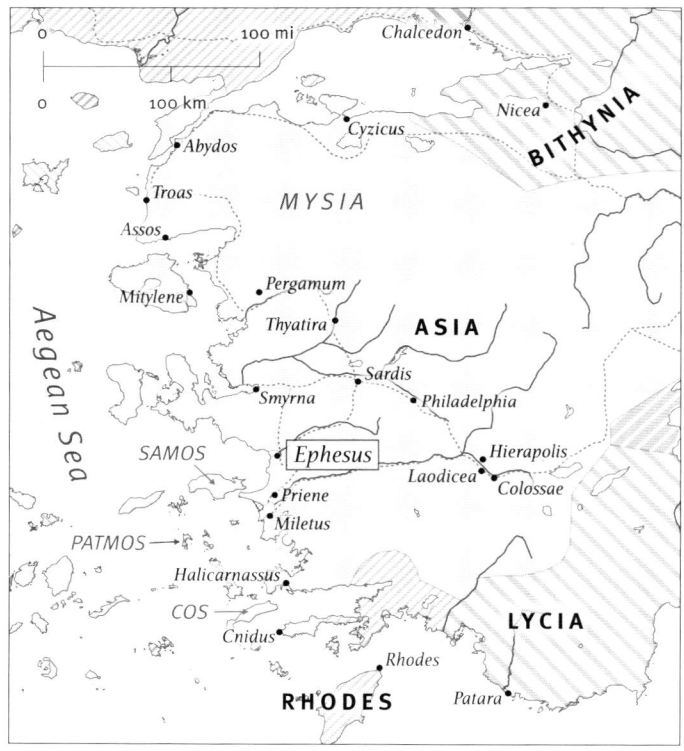

3   Map adapted from *ESV Study Bible*, 2260.

Paul's Third Missionary Journey[4]

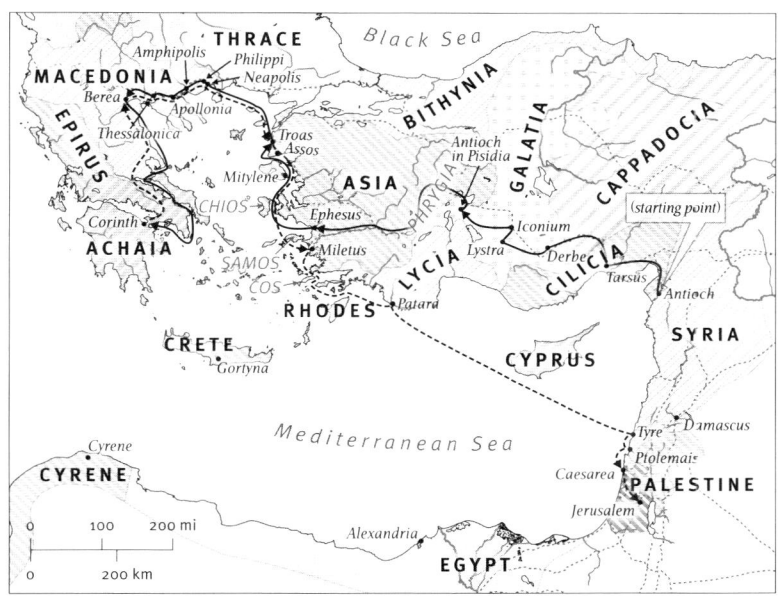

4   Map adapted from the *ESV Concise Study Bible*, ed. Paul R. House et al. (Crossway, 2021),
     1232.

General Index

Abraham, xii, 8, 38
Adam, 28
adoption, 6, 8
anger, 80, 83, 115
Apollyon, 125
apostles, 36, 39, 45, 68–69, 71–72, 78,
    103, 120
Apostles' Creed, 28, 62n1
armor, spiritual, 124–32
Artemis, xviii
authority, 99, 102–3, 112–13, 115,
    118–21, 124, 126

baptism, 45, 62–63, 97, 105
battle, 125–27, 130–32
blessings, 5–6, 8, 12
bondservants, 117–21, 123, 137
Bradford, John, 31n5
Bunyan, John, 124

calling, 48, 59, 60, 73, 94, 112–13, 120
calling, effectual, 17, 60
Carson, D. A., 54, 139
children, 39, 71–73, 77, 85–86, 88, 91,
    100–101, 111–20, 137
Christ
    ascension of, xi, 18, 28, 65–67, 69
    authority of, 9–10, 18–20, 51
    blood of, 18, 20, 35, 37
    as cornerstone of church, 37, 39
    fullness of, xvii, 21–22, 54, 70–71

as head of the church, xix, 20–21,
    62
identity in, 3, 83, 91, 100, 137
incarnation of, 66, 86
ministry of, 36, 68, 71
new life in, xix
reign of, 18–20, 66
resurrection of, xi, 18, 28–29, 65, 68
union with, 5, 28, 108
church, the, xv, xvii, xviii, 4, 20–22,
    35–39
    foundations of, 2, 39, 68, 75
    glory of, 105, 107, 126
    members of, 4, 21, 29, 33, 37–39,
        43–45, 70–71, 73–74, 79–80, 92,
        106, 135–36
circumcision, xvi, 32–33, 36
citizens, 3, 34, 38, 65, 76, 99, 112
commandments, 95, 113–114, 118n7
community, 20, 96, 135
covetousness, 86–92
creation, 9, 10, 20, 56, 63, 107–8. 113,
    114
cross, the, xvii, 2–3, 5–6, 9

darkness, 18, 48, 90–94
death, spiritual, 23–24, 26, 28, 50, 60,
    78, 103
discipline, 112, 115–16
division, 25, 33, 36, 126
doxology, 14, 17, 56–57

Scripture Index

Available from the Conversational Commentaries Series

Conversational Commentaries are designed for women leading small-group Bible studies, preparing to speak at gatherings, or seeking to deepen their understanding of God's Word. These accessible and affordable resources present the full ESV text of a specific book of the Bible, accompanied by warm, nonacademic explanations. Each volume includes an engaging introduction, historical and cultural context, key themes, and suggestions for further study. Readers will gain a deeper understanding of the book and its role in the overarching story of Scripture, ultimately growing in their knowledge of God and drawing closer to him.

For more information, visit **crossway.org**.